INFORMATIVE ASSESSMENT

In A Nutshell

s e r i e s

INFORMATIVE ASSESSMENT

When It's Not About a Grade

In A Nutshell
collection

Robin J. Fogarty • Gene M. Kerns

CORWIN
A SAGE Company

For information:

Corwin
A SAGE Company
2455 Teller Road
Thousand Oaks, California 91320
(800) 233-9936
Fax: (800) 417-2466
www.corwinpress.com

SAGE Ltd.
1 Oliver's Yard
55 City Road
London EC1Y 1SP
United Kingdom

SAGE India Pvt. Ltd.
B 1/I 1 Mohan Cooperative
    Industrial Area
Mathura Road, New Delhi 110 044
India

SAGE Asia-Pacific Pte. Ltd.
33 Pekin Street #02-01
Far East Square
Singapore 048763

Printed in the United States of America.

Library of Congress Cataloging-in-Publication Data

Fogarty, Robin J.
Informative assessment: when it's not about a grade/Robin J. Fogarty and Gene M. Kerns.
        p. cm. — (In a nutshell series)
Includes bibliographical references and index.
ISBN 978-1-4129-7542-1 (pbk.)
    1. Educational tests and measurements. 2. Effective teaching. I. Kerns, Gene M. II. Title. III. Series.

LB3051.F643 2009
371.26—dc22   2009010939

This book is printed on acid-free paper.

10   11   12   13   10   9   8   7   6   5   4   3   2

Acquisitions Editor:	Hudson Perigo
Editorial Assistant:	Lesley K. Blake
Production Editor:	Cassandra Margaret Seibel
Copy Editor:	Claire Larson
Typesetter:	C&M Digitals (P) Ltd.
Proofreader:	Marleis Roberts
Indexer:	Jean Casalegno
Cover Designer:	Anthony Paular
Graphic Designer:	Karine Hovsepian

Contents

Chapter 1
Routine Informative Assessments: Every Day—Flow   1

Chapter 3
Rigorous Informative Assessments:
Some Days — Philosophical Shift   **58**

■ □ ■ □ ■

Preface

Get the Data Right
Get the Right Data
Get the Data the Right Way
Get the Data Right Away
Get the Right Data Management

U.S. Department of Education

Referencing the adage that during his or her lifetime every person should accomplish three important tasks: plant a tree, have a child, and write a book, Ralph Tyler certainly achieved the last of the three. Ralph Tyler's book, *Basic Principles of Curriculum and Instruction* (1949), laid the groundwork for a cycle of continual, ongoing, and ever-present assessments by delineating a simple and lasting set of principles that included the following:

1. Defining appropriate learning objectives

2. Establishing useful learning experiences

3. Organizing learning experiences to have a maximum cumulative effect

4. Evaluating the curriculum and revising those aspects that do not prove to be effective

Tyler also believed that evaluation of student behaviors would be a highly appropriate means for determining educational success or failure. In fact, he first coined the term *evaluation* as it pertained to an evidence collection process that aligned to the teaching and learning process. In retrospect, the formative assessment movement has roots reaching as far back as 1949. Thus, the saying that,

"There's nothing new in education," rings true. Yet the advancement in our understanding of the concepts of formative assessment—assessment *for* learning and assessments that inform practice—is evolving rapidly as the writers, researchers, and practitioners continue the investigations. The stage is set, the players are poised and the theater patrons await the opening lines. Let the curtain rise on the play of the current day, "Informative Assessment: When It's Not About a Grade."

There's nothing new in education.

Acknowledgments

We would like to acknowledge the thinkers and researchers and writers who have influenced our treatment of formative assessment as an instrument to inform: Art Costa, Bena Kallick, Jay McTighe, Rick Stiggins, Grant Wiggins, Dylan Wiliam and Paul Black, Ken O'Connor, Howard Gardner, Doug Reeves, and Robert Marzano.

We would feel remiss if we did not acknowledge the assessment work of our dear friend and colleague, Kay Burke. She walked us through the assessment conundrum many times as we developed materials together at Skylight Training and Publishing. Her depth of knowledge and unending passion for the assessment piece in the curriculum, instruction, and assessment triangle has served us well. Our heartfelt thanks go to Kay, a caring educator and longtime partner in all things academic.

Dedications

To Brian, my source of strength and calm—Robin

To the many educators in my family of birth, and to Dean, the center of my family of choice—Gene

About the Authors

Robin J. Fogarty, Ph.D., is president of Robin Fogarty and Associates, Ltd., a Chicago-based, minority-owned, educational publishing and consulting company. Her doctorate is in curriculum and human resource development from Loyola University of Chicago. A leading proponent of the thoughtful classroom, Robin has trained educators throughout the world in curriculum, instruction, and assessment strategies. She has taught at all levels, from kindergarten to college, served as an administrator, and consulted with state departments and ministries of education in the United States, Puerto Rico, Russia, Canada, Australia, New Zealand, Germany, Great Britain, Singapore, Korea, and the Netherlands. Robin has published articles in *Educational Leadership, Phi Delta Kappan,* and the *Journal of Staff Development.* She is the author of numerous publications, including *Brain-Compatible Classrooms, Ten Things New Teachers Need to Succeed, Literacy Matters: Strategies Every Teacher Can Use, How to Integrate the Curricula, The Adult Learner, A Look at Transfer, Close the Achievement Gap: Strategies That Work, Twelve Brain Principles That Make the Difference, Nine Best Practices That Make the Difference,* and *From Staff Room to Classroom: A Guide to Planning and Coaching Professional Learning.*

 **Gene M. Kerns, Ed.D.,** is a third-generation educator with teaching experience from elementary through the university level, in addition to K–12 administrative experience. Gene serves as vice president of training and certification for Renaissance Learning, Inc. With more than a decade of experience in leading professional development sessions, as well as taking on the role of presenter at national and international conferences, Gene has knowledge and know-how of the adult learner. In addition, he has the experience to work across the generations with a genuine quality that is laced with anecdotes, humor, and heartfelt passion. Former clients include the New York State Unified Teachers, New Jersey Principals' Association, Illinois Coalition of Essential Schools, and the Ministry of Education of Singapore. Gene received his bachelor's and master's degrees from Longwood College in Virginia. He also holds a doctor of education degree from the University of Delaware, with an emphasis in education leadership. *inFormative Assessment: When It's Not About a Grade* is Gene's first publication.

Introduction

Part I: Purpose and Goals

Purpose: Changing of the Guard

The overriding purpose of this little In a Nutshell book, *inFormative Assessment: When It's Not About a Grade*, is to provide a research-based, teacher-friendly resource. This valuable book features a spectrum of formative assessment tools and techniques to help the teacher assess student work and academic progress in an ongoing, continuous, and consistent manner.

It's a given that academic assessments inform. What is not as obvious is whether that information is received early enough and then utilized judiciously to guide and enhance instruction. That, in essence, is the fundamental difference between traditional views of assessment and the emergent view of the current formative assessment.

The key to this at-a-glance guide is to demonstrate how these many tools and techniques are available for assessment purposes, as well as for quality instruction. One might think about the informative assessment piece in this paradoxical view: Instructional practices often serve as assessment practices. Assessment practices often serve as instructional practices. Or, put more succinctly, instruction is assessment; assessment is instruction. The two are intertwined within the complexities of the quality K–12 classroom.

> **Instructional practices often serve as assessment practices. Assessment practices often serve as instructional practices.**

Goals

The goals are twofold: (1) to present practical tools and proven techniques for the K–12 classroom teacher that can be woven into the very fabric of the instructional day and (2) to empower students with understanding and insight about how they learn and how they might expand their capacities as lifelong learners.

The assessment tools highlighted often serve as instructional instruments, as well as yield assessment information. The techniques are often aligned with best practices that work across the grain of the K–12 classroom. Some tools are familiar to those involved in quality teaching; some tools may be completely new, or they may just add a new twist to an old tool.

Empowering students with understanding and insight about their own power to learn is the second goal. This process of true empowerment dictates the skillful and robust use of formative assessments as part and parcel of the teaching and learning equation.

Part II: A Suite of Informative Assessments Practices

Formative Assessments and Summative Assessments

When the chef tastes the soup, it's formative!
When the customer tastes the soup, it's summative!

Black and Wiliam (1998), as cited by Brookhart (1999), as cited by Swearingen (2002)

Instruction and assessment go hand in hand. In fact, assessments inform instruction with both formative and summative data. The striking difference between assessment *of* instruction and assessment *for* instruction is found in the following two questions. Assessment *of* instruction asks, *How did I do?* while assessment *for* instruction asks, *How am I doing?* Summative assessments provide data for grades and rankings at the end point of the instruction. Formative data inform instructional practice as it is happening and when there is still time to make the needed adjustments in order to facilitate student learning.

Formative Assessments

Informative Assessment: Genesis of the Term

Much of the current interest in formative assessment was sparked by Paul Black and Dylan Wiliam's landmark 1998 work, "Inside the Black Box," a meta-analysis of research on assessment that revealed two major findings: (1) "students taught by teachers who integrated assessment with instruction could achieve in six or seven months what would otherwise take a year" and (2) that "these improvements appear to be consistent across countries . . . across ages and across subjects" (Black & Wiliam, 1998, pp. 21).

The profundity of these findings then sparked the authors and many others around the globe (most notably in the United States, Rick Stiggins and his colleagues at the Assessment Training Institute) to begin to explore the nature of assessment strategies that promote learning. All of this has occurred as high-stakes, high-accountability assessments have risen in prominence and "diverted attention [from the] more important and fundamental purpose" of improving student learning (Guskey, 2003, p. 11).

Seeking to delineate this assessment initiative and to develop assessments that promote learning from the use of assessments as accountability tools, authors have sought an appropriate term to describe this type of assessment. Some refer to them under the well-known banner of "formative assessments," advancing that the moment a score or rank becomes attached, the assessment becomes summative and loses its power to promote learning. Others describe this subset of assessments as assessments *for*

learning, as opposed to summative assessments *of* learning, whose purpose is to rank and rate.

> *Because that standardized testing light has been so brilliant in our eyes, we haven't seen past it to another application of assessment in schools that promises even greater impact on student learning. This is the classroom level of assessment. We have neglected to put into place day-to-day classroom assessment practices that set both teachers and students up for success, and that's a crisis.*
>
> There are the success-oriented students and they win the system, and the failure-accepting students and they don't. One of those groups has already met standards and the other hasn't. (Assessment Training Institute, 2003)

We have chosen to focus on the function of assessments rather than their form, using the term *informative assessment* because what we are really seeking are assessments that inform teachers and students. For example, data from summative tests can be used in a very formative manner to help students self-analyze, review, and re-test. In this case, the form is summative but the use is formative—it informs the student.

Typically, formative assessments exhibit some or all of the following characteristics. Formative assessments are usually ongoing and classroom-based, somewhat momentary, or fleeting glances, and many times self-evaluative and self-reflective. Formative assessments inform. They are utilized to provide relevant, timely, and maximum feedback on student learning. They are, more often than not, not about a grade! Rather, formative assessments are about providing guideposts that keep the learning moving forward and on track. Informative assessments must inform teacher practice, but more importantly, informative assessments can also inform the students of their level of understanding as a personal appraisal, as opposed to their standings in the class roster.

These informative assessments range from cueing questions and feedback techniques to common checks for understanding to activating prior knowledge. Informative assessments are often regarded as "soft" data that is available, accessible, and attainable within the internal workings of the classroom.

Illustrations of formative assessments include such things as teacher observation, peer reviews, anecdotal records, student work samples, pop quizzes, and student portfolios.

Formative assessments provide ongoing and, often, just-in-time data on student progress.

Formative assessments provide ongoing and, often, just-in-time data on student progress.

This formative data truly informs many of the stakeholders, students, peers, and teachers about the depth of understanding students are experiencing. In turn, it often dictates adjustments and changes to correct the course to enhance student learning.

Summative Assessments

Summative assessments are used to indicate the sum of what has been learned in a particular endeavor. Summative assessments imply that there is an accumulation of evidence that indicates the extent of the learning. Summative data are utilized to classify, categorize, and label learners for future placements. They are, more often than not, definitely about a grade, whether it be pass/fail, a letter grade, or a numerical rendering.

These summative assessments range from standardized test scores to end-of-course tests, from weekly essays to pop quizzes. Summative assessments are often regarded as "hard" data that yield grades, scores, or rankings. Summative assessments must provide the quantitative data used to calculate grade point averages, school rankings, and district placement on state and national norms.

Examples of summative assessments often include normative assessments, such as nationally standardized tests, criterion–referenced tests (such as end-of-chapter or state tests based on the content standards), and end-of-course tests that certify learning in a particular course of study. Summative assessments typically provide scores and rankings that are used in developing demographic data and statistics. However, these traditionally summative assessments can also provide information that can be used formatively. There will be more on the concept of summative assessments used for formative purposes in subsequent chapters.

A Suite of Informative Assessment Practices

In this teacher-friendly discussion, the reader learns about teacher-tested, tried and true informative assessment tools to use when it's not about the grade, but rather when it's about learning. They can apply these tools immediately in their K–12 classrooms. This suite of informative assessments is composed of a set of appraisal tools, techniques, and tips, accompanied by teachings and tasks. They are organized around three levels of implementation that encompass routine kinds of things the teacher can do all day, every day, to more rigorous analytical tools that are plotted more deliberately. Thus these are appropriately labeled *routine, reflective,* and *rigorous informative assessments.*

1. Routine Informative Assessments weave into everyday classroom instruction *all day, every day.*

2. Reflective Informative Assessments foster self-assessment for students and teachers and are used *many days* during the term.

3. Rigorous Informative Assessments provide constant and continual professional learning to inform teaching practices and student learning and are used on *some days,* designated for design and development.

Routine Informative Assessments weave into everyday classroom instruction and are used all day, every day, throughout the term or semester. These strategies are simple things that skillful teachers do to monitor and assess student learning on a daily, task-to-task, lesson-to-lesson, or unit-to-unit basis. This is truly assessment for information, informing the teacher and helping to direct the instructional plan. Routine Informative Assessment moves beyond the traditional, "teach/assess/grade cycle" of times past. This routine assessment's purpose is solely informative. It is not about the grade; it is about the goal.

> **Routine Informative Assessments weave into everyday classroom instruction.**

A sampling of strategies included in this compendium of best practices ranges from simple signals and response strategies to maximize feedback from the students to a reversal strategy on student questions—clearly not an exhaustive listing, yet these items do provide a glimpse at this category of informative assessments.

- Check for understanding signals

- Wait time strategy

- Delving questions

- Unpacking the language of the task

- Hands up only to ask a question

Reflective Informative Assessments foster self-assessment for students and teachers, not necessarily every day, but *many days*, to accentuate and accelerate the learning. Frequently, during a lesson or throughout the unit of study, reflective techniques are purposefully incorporated to foster self-appraisal and self-awareness about what the students know and what they don't know yet. These tools promote deeper,

> **Reflective techniques are purposefully incorporated to foster self-appraisal and self-awareness.**

more enduring learning for students. The strategies are designed as a metacognitive approach to lifelong learning, with an emphasis on learning to learn skills that illuminate, the how-to-learn aspect of the learning process. This set of tools and techniques is deliberately factored into the classroom instructional map, to ensure learning for a lifetime, not just learning for the test.

Highlighted in this section is a spectrum of practical ideas that range from anticipation guides that tap into prior knowledge and background experiences to post-learning formats for checking for understanding and for analyzing the quality of student work.

- Agree/disagree discussion guides

- The human graph (take a stand)

- Range-finding and hinge-point questions

- Student portfolios

- Checklists and rubrics

Rigorous assessment techniques provide constant and continual professional learning that informs teaching practices.

Rigorous Informative Assessments, unlike the previous two categories of informative assessment tools, focus on developing the teachers' knowledge and understanding of assessment tools. While the end user is always the student, these more rigorous assessment techniques provide constant and continual professional learning that informs teaching practices first. Of course, subsequently, these tools benefit students by impacting positively on their achievement. Rigorous assessments, as presented in the following discussions, are distinguished by the attribute of complexity. The tools, techniques, and tips delineated in this category often require focused effort in addition to and aside from the instructional time allotted within the schedule. Teachers may need specifically scheduled meetings that target development of these ideas.

Featured in this set of Rigorous Informative Assessments are ideas that run the gamut from robust performance tasks to grading practices that make the data more accessible to item analysis techniques and test creation. It is becoming more obvious with this rigorous genre of informative assessments why, more often than not, teachers may need dedicated time to fully unpack them and understand how to use them.

- Performance tasks

- Color-coded grade books

- Item analysis-robust distracters

- Test creation software

- Using summative assessment to inform

Part III: Background and Research

The role of assessment in the instructional arena harkens back to Ralph Tyler (1949) and his classic, *Basic Principles of Curriculum and Instruction,* in which he declares the triad of curriculum, instruction, and assessment inextricably linked. This seminal piece is still the foundation of much of the academic thinking, planning, and designing that occurs in the field today. Below is a delineation of numerous others who have contributed to the accumulated wisdom about assessment that is so pervasive in today's schools.

The role of assessment in the instructional arena harkens back to Ralph Tyler.

Research and Theory Base
Black and Wiliam (1998)

Known for their seminal piece, "Inside the Black Box," the authors posit that the classroom is treated like a black box.

They question the model in which inputs are fed in (pupils, teachers, parent demands) and some outputs follow (student knowledge and competencies). They posit further that teaching and learning have to be interactive, in ways that teachers know about student progress so adjustments can be made along the way. In short, they make the case for formative assessments used to adapt the teaching work to meet the needs.

Burke (2004)

Standards to checklists to rubrics is the mantra that Burke advocates, as she models how to dissect the exact language of the standard of learning and construct straightforward checklists of skills. In turn, she then demonstrates how to move the checklist into a scoring rubric with quality indicators.

Costa (2000)

Assessing "intelligent behavior" (the predecessor to *Discovering & Exploring Habits of Mind*), in a metacognitive way, is the heart and soul of Costa's work. His robust, reflective assessment concepts have emerged over the span of an illustrious career that focused on educational leadership, higher order thinking, intelligent behaviors, and ongoing reflective assessments.

Dweck (2007)

Carol Dweck makes a case for and against praise. She proposes that the wrong kind of praise (praise on intelligence-smart, ability) can create self-defeating behaviors, while the right kind of praise (praise on process and effort-engagement, perseverance, strategies, improvement) motivated students to learn. Her work is in this area of attribution theory and concerns motivation, personality, and development.

Gardner (1983)

Founder and creator of the theory of multiple intelligences, Gardner changed the way we looked at assessment, by adding an "s" to the word "intelligence." He favors a profile of assessments that tap into the eight distinct arenas of the intelligent mind: verbal, visual, interpersonal, intrapersonal, mathematical, musical, naturalist, and bodily/kinesthetic.

Guskey (2007)

Focused on grading practices and assessments that are formative in nature, Guskey promotes a highly practical approach to grades and grading. His view aligns with the informative assessment philosophy. Grades and gradings are necessary in classrooms, but their higher purpose should be to inform and alert students for revised action and to inform professional practice.

Kallick (2000)

Coauthor of *Discovering & Exploring Habits of Mind* with Art Costa, Kallick has been an advocate for assessment planning. She promotes a series of different types of assessments to inform teaching practices. Known historically for promoting the idea of a "system of assessments," rather than a singular assessment tactic, Kallick advocates developmentally appropriate materials, tasks, and assessment strategies for students, based on their readiness levels.

Marzano, Pickering, and McTighe (1993)

Authors of an early work on scoring rubrics aligned to student learning standards, the concepts of Marzano, Pickering, and McTighe have developed into a system of using rubrics to accompany performances and projects. Whether developed by the teacher or with the students, the rubrics delineate key elements that indicate adherence to the standards.

O'Connor (2002)

How to Grade for Learning shows how to link grades and standards through eight models. These strategies assist teachers in designing and conducting grading practices that help students feel more in control of their academic success. O'Connor was among the first to delineate practical examples of how to grade for learning, not just for the record book.

Popham (2006)

Testing and its uses and abuses are ongoing themes of Popham's work. He abhors the reliance schools have placed on normed tests and urges educators to use the information gleaned from these tests in responsible and reliable ways. All testing should benefit the teaching and learning process, according to Popham. While he often writes about these nationally normed tests, he also writes about formative assessments or classroom assessments. He believes these should be regarded as a process, not a point-in-time score.

Reeves (2008)

Reeves's work in the area of grading practices is well known in the educational community. His sometimes radical statements, such as "No averages of scores for the semester" and "No zeros for missing work" and "No one killer assignment for the semester," illustrate how high-stakes grading practices make a difference. Based on standards and assessments, steps can be taken to make grading practices supportive rather than punitive.

Stiggins (2007)

Assessment for learning is the hallmark of the pioneering and ongoing work of Rick Stiggins. He is responsible for promoting the formative assessment movement in the educational community, and his influence continues. In fact, his work has been a trademark in schools, as they continue the shift from sole reliance on summative assessments to a synchronized effort to bring formative assessments on the scene in truly meaningful ways.

Wiggins and McTighe (2005)

Understanding by Design is the simple yet complex concept that promotes the idea of designing learning with the end in mind. Backward mapping is at the heart of this model, which emphasizes teaching for "enduring learnings," as well as for needed content-based skills and concepts. Designing with the end in mind places the "results" or assessments, front and center.

Part IV: Overview of Book and Chapters

About the Book Format

The In a Nutshell Book, *inFormative Assessments: When It's Not About a Grade,* is intended for classroom teachers, teacher leaders, mentors, coaches, and school leadership. It is designed to be a substantive yet succinct discussion on the topic of formative assessments and the role of assessment for learning, in the teaching and learning cycle.

The discussion is research-based, the tone is conversational, the ideas are practical and the intent is results oriented. While readers will know the voices in the field who are writing and researching on this subject, they will also see the indelible imprint of classroom teachers who are inventing and using powerful and practical tools and techniques to achieve the goal of assessments that *inform.*

The following chapters include introductory material to set the scene and several chapters that help categorize the informative assessment strategies. These chapters include Routine Informative Assessments, to weave into everyday classroom instruction; Reflective Informative Assessments, to foster self-assessment for students and for teachers; and Rigorous Informative Assessments, to provide constant and continual professional learning tools that inform teaching practices and student learning.

The book ends with a closure discussion dedicated to the overriding concept that informative assessment celebrates: student success, as presented by Carol Dweck's attribution theory, and its relationship to student attitude and confidence.

About the Chapter Format

The three major chapters are formatted consistently throughout the book. Each informative assessment chapter presents five elements that help the reader maneuver the pages with ease and grace. These key chapters have five sections: Teachings, Tools, Techniques, Tasks, and Tips. Let's look a little closer at each of these to examine exactly what might be included in the sections.

Teachings

This opening section sets the context with definitions, descriptions, explanations, and examples. This is the introduction and information that unveils the rest of the chapter ideas. This is the "surround sound" that supports the more nitty-gritty, practical pieces.

Tools

These are hands-on manipulatives, games, puzzles, guides, quick references that are teacher-tested, tried-and-true classroom instruments that help students learn, as well as help them learn how to learn. They are objects promoting assessment processes.

Techniques

Similar to the tools above, yet different; the techniques section includes methods, methodology, and the ways and means of using assessment to drive instructional decisions. These are processes that manifest various and sundry formative assessments.

Tasks

The tasks section presents actual applications to try, and real, authentic uses gleaned from classroom teachers who are finding that student success is enhanced by these measures. The tasks delineate ideas for immediate transfer to the K–12 classroom.

Tips

The final element in each chapter consists of clues and cues—hints, if you will—from experts on what, when, and how to use the information successfully. This section houses the coaching piece, the seasoned voice, any words of wisdom that seem warranted.

Chapter 1

Routine Informative Assessments
Every Day—Flow

SCENARIO (Reader's Theater)

All Day, Every Day!

The scene is Star Middle School, with a new teacher, Ms. Juarez, and a veteran teacher, Mr. Brant. This is taking place during their lunch break, and they are talking about a math lesson that had occurred earlier that morning. Their discussion centers on student involvement and feedback during a lesson in Ms. Juarez's class.

Ms. Juarez

We just had a great discussion in my geometry class this morning about how to develop proofs for theorems. A couple of students dialogued back and forth for a few minutes and really seemed to understand the key strategies to use. My concern is that the rest of the students were not that engaged. They were attentive and they looked like they were listening, but I really don't know what they know or what they don't know.

Mr. Brant

As part and parcel of my lessons, I use a host of strategies to get feedback during those lessons. I want to know if it "takes" or not. I want to know if the kids really get it or if they're lost. I use a whole array of formative assessments to get that feedback.

Ms. Juarez

Formative assessments? I'm not sure what you mean by that, but I do assess the class after the lesson. I usually use those tests for a grade in the grade book. It gives me a read on where they are on that skill or concept.

Mr. Brant

Well, these kinds of assessment are a little different. They are more like touchbacks, to get immediate feedback during the lesson itself. Formative assessments inform. They are the ways I use to find out if the kids are on track with the lesson or if they need another swing at it.

Ms. Juarez

Oh, I see what you mean. Formative assessments are like check points along the way.

Mr. Brant

That's right. I even call these assessments "informative assessments," rather than formative assessments, to make the point very clear that they are used to inform. In fact, they are not about a grade at all. They are tools and techniques I use all day long, every day, to maximize feedback from students.

Ms. Juarez

That's exactly what I think was missing from the dialogue this morning. It was just between the two kids. While I felt they did have a good understanding of the lesson, I was not sure how everyone else had fared.

Mr. Brant

Exactly! That's my point. We need student feedback, *all day, every day,* to temper our lesson accordingly.

Ms. Juarez

Would you tell me more about this idea of informative assessments if I come by after school? I would love to have some concrete ideas that I could use right away in my classes.

Mr. Brant

Absolutely! Come by after school, and I will show you some tools and techniques I use all of the time. They are part of all of my lessons. In fact, I guess you could say that these assessments are woven into the lessons. The instruction and assessments are seamless. They occur almost simultaneously, with quick checks throughout the lesson, to be sure all the students are on board.

Ms. Juarez

I can't wait to talk more! I'll be down as soon as the kids are gone, today.

Mr. Brant

Okay! I'll get some things together for you. See you later.

Teachings

Defining Routine Informative Assessments

To define the concept of Routine Informative Assessments, it is necessary to unpack the word *routine*. *Routine,* in the context of classroom instruction, means standard things that occur, tactics or strategies, performed with regularity, as part of the day-to-day occurrences. In brief, routine refers to happenings that fit into the scheme of things on a daily basis. All day long, every day of the week, these Routine Informative Assessments occur as an essential part of the lesson or review.

> *Routine,* in the context of classroom instruction, means standard things that occur.

Routine Informative Assessment is to be interpreted as the daily "activities undertaken by the teachers and/or by their students, which provide information to be used as feedback to modify the teaching and learning activities in which they are engaged" (Black & Wiliam, 1998, p. 142).

Describing Routine Informative Assessments

Routinely, these assessment strategies are woven into the daily schedule of instructional events and are inexplicably linked to the instructional tenor of the classroom. They are simple, repetitious assessment strategies, threaded throughout the instruction. The purpose is to inform, to provide immediate, continual, and valuable feedback from students that signals a need for adjustments and modifications in the instruction.

To that end, maximizing student feedback, Routine Informative Assessments become a regular and integral part of the instructional scene. In fact, these are as routine as taking attendance or lunch count, setting classroom rules, or assigning homework. Routine Informative Assessments are as common to good classrooms as building vocabulary in each lesson or unit, or checking math calculations for accuracy. These all-day, everyday assessments are as routine as the communication skills of reading, writing, speaking, and listening. They are, indeed, part and parcel of the moment-to-moment, hour-to-hour, lesson-to-lesson dynamics of the quality K–12 classroom.

> **Routine Informative Assessments . . . are as routine as taking attendance or lunch count, setting classroom rules, or assigning homework.**

Examples of Routine Assessments That Inform

First and foremost, Routine Informative Assessments are the routine. These kinds of assessments include a number of strategic measures that teachers regularly use within the discourse of the classroom interactions. Among the most frequently used routine assessments that inform instructional practice are student response devices. These are strategies to foster equal opportunity for response and robust, varied, and effective questioning and response strategies.

More specifically, student response devices can be handmade and handheld signal cards or more sophisticated portable, electronic devices that signal agreement, disagreement, or multiple-choice answers. Strategies that promote equal opportunity for responses among all students in the class or in the group include name cards, a deck of cards, a fishbowl kind of name drawing, or even color-coded tongue depressors with student names on them. Robust questioning strategies include rhetorical and woven questions, as well as more complex questions for probing and delving for more comprehensive and revealing responses.

In the next several sections of the chapter, titled Tools, Techniques, Tasks, and Tips, this set of routine assessments will be delineated more fully. Each is explained comprehensively, examples are drawn, an activity for immediate use is included, and tips are given to clarify the implementation processes. Of course, the goal is to motivate practical application of these vital assessment ideas to improve classroom practices.

For clarification, the distinction made between tools and techniques is a deliberate one. *Tools* are often objects and manipulatives, specific instruments that can be used in the classroom for immediate and relevant student feedback. They are often reusable and become an integral part of the daily instructional methodology.

On the other hand, *techniques* comprise more intricate tactics and strategies. Routine Informative Assessment techniques are often customized and tailored to the specific teaching and learning situation. Techniques may vary in their targeted use by complexity, intensity, and duration, depending on the particular instructional circumstance.

The *tasks* are selected to demonstrate an immediate application, while the *tips* assist with the *whys* and *wherefores* of actual implementation in K–12 classrooms. In the end, these last sections of the chapter are intended to lead the reader to clearer understandings by illustrations of actual applications.

Tools

Routine Handmade Tools

One of the easiest and most frequently used sets of tools is gathered here under the heading of handmade tools. These simple, low-tech tools are easily obtained or created by the classroom teacher. These are tools used by teachers who are focused on maximizing student feedback through multiple opportunities to respond and through signaling devices that make those responses visible and assessable. Among the listing of handmade tools for maximizing feedback are traffic light cards, color-coded multiple choice cards, individual lap boards, tongue depressors, name cards, and a deck of cards.

These simple, low-tech tools are easily obtained or created by the classroom teacher.

Traffic Light Cards

Traffic light cards consist of three cards that simulate the traffic light: green, yellow, and red. As the teacher proceeds with the lesson, students are prompted to self-assess their understanding at that point and signal:

> *Green—Go! I'm on board* (teacher notes and continues if majority are okay)

> *Yellow—Slow down! I'm coming* (teacher pauses, student collaborates)

> *Red—Stop! I'm confused* (teacher clarifies concern and adapts accordingly by reteaching the whole group if necessary, pulling a small group aside for a new approach, or making adjustments for the next lesson step that is needed)

Color-Coded Multiple Choice Cards

Using three or four letter-coded cards (A, B, C, D), students are engaged and involved as they signal their choice for options displayed by the teacher. This is an effective way to begin a lesson (prior knowledge), to use during the lesson (monitoring key concepts), and at the end of a lesson (checking for understanding).

Lap Boards

Lap boards may be individual white boards, blackboards, or magnetic (Etch-a-Sketch) boards, but in all cases, the students use the boards to signal a response to the posed question. Teachers utilize this tool for mental math drills (3×12), spelling drills (*rhyming words*) comprehension questions (*to which character do you relate the most?*), concept development (*symbol for carbon dioxide*), or even simple classification knowledge (*name a type of rock*).

Tongue Depressors

Simple tongue depressors, or color-coded tongue depressors, serve as tools for a well-researched phenomenon that occurs in typical classrooms. The concept of equal opportunity to respond is part of the Teacher Expectation, Student Achievement Study (Kerman, 1979), which calls attention to the inadvertent teacher behavior of consistently calling on the same students rather than ensuring every student the opportunity to answer. By using tongue depressors with students' names on them, the teacher has a structure to guide this process and allow all students a chance to respond.

Name Cards and Fishbowl

Name cards are similar to the tongue depressor tool. The names of students are placed in a fishbowl, and the teacher randomly draws names throughout the lesson. In essence, the concept of *equal opportunity to respond* is activated. According to the research cited earlier, this modified teacher behavior of promoting and expecting responses from all students is part of the process of setting high expectations for all learners.

Routine Electronic Tools

The idea of maximizing feedback has developed into a viable and desirable strategy for the quality classroom. Thus, in addition to the aforementioned homemade responders, technology solutions are also available for many schools, currently focused on integrating technology into the curriculum. While two such devices are described here, they are by no means the only ones on the market or in the schools. Yet, for the techno-savvy, these electronic responders are compelling tools for today's classrooms.

Responders or "2Know!"

Classroom response systems like Renaissance Learning's "2Know!" encourage engagement and are powerful tools for teachers to use to maximize feedback. Teachers pose questions, verbally or on a screen, students respond, and the system instantly processes and graphs the responses. While teachers can use various low-tech options outlined herein (e.g., response cards), one indisputable benefit of response systems is that they allow students to respond with anonymity. Additionally, they are more accurate. While a teacher would have to approximate correct response rates through low-tech options, the use of response systems allows the teacher to view exact data on the students' responses.

NEO 2

Another tool, in the form of a compact, portable keyboard device, is the NEO 2, produced by Renaissance Learning. While this is an effective and affordable classroom tool for learning keyboarding and writing, it also serves as a student responder device. Students log in and respond much like they do with a simple response system. Additionally, NEO 2 creates a mini classroom network, allowing students to print work through the teacher's workstation and share their assignments efficiently with peers and their teacher.

Routine Questioning Tools

There are two question sets that easily become part and parcel of the classroom questioning toolbox. One set of questions urges students to elaborate on their thinking with more depth by giving specific illustrations of their thinking, and the other set prompts students to access prior knowledge for greater comprehension.

Mr. Pete's Questions

One of the simplest and most straightforward tools for routinely assessing student thinking is a set of questions called Mr. Pete's Questions, which were developed by Brian Pete. These questions are follow-up questions to a student response that usually elicit a whole paragraph of meaning. For example, after a student has offered a one-word response to the question posed by the teacher, the teacher follows up with the following:

Teacher Response 1: Tell me more.

Teacher Response 2: Can you give me an example of that?

Teacher Response 3: How do you feel about that?

Notice that each of the follow-up questions builds on the previous one. But please also note that the teacher may choose to use any or all three of the follow-up questions.

Mr. Parnes' Questions

Mr. Parnes' Questions originated with Sidney Parnes, of Buffalo State College. Parnes advocated these two questions as a way to take learning to a new level. Indeed, by helping students access these simple tools, teachers will dictate a higher level of thinking about the new learning.

Question 1: How does this connect to something you already know?

Question 2: How might you use this in the future?

By activating prior knowledge and by pushing for transfer, use, and relevant application, Mr. Parnes' Questions are questions that can be used all day, every day, to prompt self-assessment as well as teacher observational assessments. By virtue of the questions themselves, there is enough student feedback to alter the instructional focus for certain students if warranted.

Techniques

Included in this section are techniques to utilize classroom questioning and response strategies, cooperative learning techniques, teacher expectations, and vocabulary to inform instruction. These forms of assessment are designated as techniques or strategies, as they vary greatly within the context of their applications. Yet these techniques are intended to provide valued information to the students and the teacher about their mastery of the material.

Questioning techniques move from higher-order thinking questions, which probe and delve for more depth, to new ways to think about questions to spark discussion. Cooperative structures are addressed with some detail to rules and routines that elicit more involvement and engagement from all students. Finally, the idea of teacher expectations and basic verbal skills are discussed in terms of providing evidence-based work for informative assessment purposes.

Routine HOT Questioning Techniques

To begin this important discussion about questioning strategies as powerful techniques for ascertaining student knowledge and understanding, there are several protocols that seem to guide the art of the classroom questioning process. These are often seen as part of the quality instructional scene in every classroom around the world.

They include the following four simple behaviors:

1. Pose the question.

   Use open-ended, divergent questions that allow various responses, based on reasoning and logic.

2. Allow wait time.

   Pause three to ten seconds after posing the question; allow time for students to think and compose a worthy response.

3. Choose a respondent using a random method.

   Revisit the tools section above and use one of the ideas provided to give the opportunity for all students to respond.

4. Provide some "save face" option!

   Let students confer and explore answers together before they offer responses. Maybe ask for no hands up, with the understanding that all students should be prepared to respond, at all times (Black, Harrison, Lee, Marshall, & Wiliam, 2003).

With that in mind, let's take a more philosophical look at questioning techniques that provide Routine Informative Assessments for the knowing teacher. Art Costa has said teachers actually dictate the level of thinking by the kinds of questions they ask (Costa & Kallick, 2000). Along the same line of thought, another great thinker, Oliver Wendell Holmes, frames the questioning issue in a stunning metaphor, known as "The Three Story Intellect."

> [There are] [o]ne-story intellects, two-story intellects, three-story intellects with skylights. All fact collectors, who have no aim beyond their facts, are one-story [minds]. Two-story [minds] compare, reason, generalize, using the labors of the fact collectors as well as their own. Three-story [minds] idealize,

imagine, predict; their best illumination comes from above, through the skylight.

—Oliver Wendell Holmes, *The Poet at the Breakfast-Table* (p. 44)

Using the concept of the three-story intellect as a guide, teachers frame their questioning with rigor and richness. In turn, students frame their responses with equal rigor and richness. The level of discourse is truly guided by the question stimulus.

As a side note, there is an easy way to think about higher-level questions. The technique uses the idea of fat and skinny questions to designate divergent questions from convergent questions. It is a technique that helps teachers and students alike. It gives them an easy way to talk about the levels of student response. *Fat questions* require elaboration to answer. They need a whole-paragraph response, while *skinny questions* demand a simple "yes," "no," or "maybe so." It's just another look at the idea of raising the level of the classroom discourse for informative assessment data.

Rhetorical Questions

The use of rhetorical questions during an input session is the first level of interaction. Rhetorical questions punctuate the lecture with a moment to pause and think about what has just been presented. For example, a rhetorical question such as "Wouldn't you agree?" causes the listener to respond mentally. The internal pause to think and to react is internal, but nonetheless, it creates just the slightest bit of interactivity. Again, the purpose is not to elicit an actual recordable response, but simply to garner a personal reaction.

A rhetorical question such as "Wouldn't you agree?" causes the listener to respond mentally.

The rhetorical question may be revisited. "Remember when I asked you if you agreed with my theses? Would anyone be willing to share that thought with the rest of us?" This is a glimpse at reactions that is an emerging form of formative assessment. It gives a little notion of what students might be thinking.

Woven Questions

Woven questions are just that. They are often directed to a particular student. They are deliberate and purposeful and are literally woven into the lecture for the explicit purpose of creating a conversation: "Derek, what is one aspect of Watson's theory that bothers you?" Whatever the response, both the teacher and students have a reading on the situation. The teacher may also follow up with a second student, to make the feedback more plentiful: "Amy, how do you feel about what Derek just said?" Both questions are woven into the lecture scenario, are open-ended, and provide a form of feedback that illuminates the learning.

Probing

Probing questions push the learner to go further, to elaborate, to give more detail, add more depth. The questions probe for clarification of various facets of an idea. A probing question often follows an initial question. The following are examples:

Teacher:

"Dee, do you believe we have environmental issues about climate changes?"

Student:

"Yes, I have seen lots of stuff in the news and documentaries about this."

Teacher:

"Can you give us some telling details that distinguish your concerns about the environment and climate change?"

Student:

"Well, I know there is a thing called global warming, that is melting the icebergs and putting the polar bears at risk."

Notice how the probing question got to specific information that illustrates the problem. This is what the skillful teacher uses to probe for the level of understanding.

Delving

Delving is another strategy that takes questioning to a deeper level. To delve is to go deeper into a fact or a piece of data. It unpacks the idea with further relevant information. For example, the teacher may use delving questions to target the goal of a project. An example that comes to mind occurred in a second grade classroom. The teacher was integrating a science unit on energy and matter with a language arts lesson on narratives. After reading the story about "The Pudding Night," the students were busy making pudding. They were shaking a container with instant pudding powder and water to turn it into pudding. When the teacher asked the students what they were doing, they replied, "Making pudding." Then she delved deeper by saying, "Yes, that's true. But can you explain how making pudding helps us understand the idea of changes in the state of matter?" By delving deeper with the class, their connections will be revealing of their understanding of the science behind the pudding theme.

Reverse Questioning Policy

Another questioning idea that may be new on the scene is the "reverse question policy" used to stimulate student-asked questions. With the "hands up only to ask a question" policy, a subtle message is being relayed to students: No need to raise your hands, as everyone is expected to be ready to respond to my questions, and there are cooperative structures in place to help everyone feel prepared; however, if you want to pose a question for the rest of us, you may raise your hand to do so. Surely, the posed questions will help guide instructional decisions as students reveal what they are thinking about. It is yet another way to get feedback for informative assessment purposes. It is a policy that will evolve over time, as kids become more comfortable with the changes in expected interactions.

Routine Informal Cooperative Learning Techniques

Cooperative learning, all day, every day, is a powerful and often underused strategy to provide Routine Informative Assessment information. It is also the number one strategy to increase student achievement and self-esteem (Johnson & Johnson, 1988).

In addition, it is an effective and versatile way to make your lecture, stand-up teaching, or whole-class instruction more interactive. The following are three simple, quick and slick ways to advocate interactive feedback for assessing student understanding.

"Turn to Your Partner, and . . ." (TTYPA . . .)

"Turn to your partner, and . . ." (TTYPA . . .) is an amazing strategy that is used in lecture halls across the nation. It is the pause on the commentary that allows students to make sense of the flow of incoming data. Once students have had a moment or two to talk, the teacher may sample a few comments for valued feedback.

Shoulder Partner

By using the same TTYPA . . . strategy, with the idea of a shoulder partner, teachers can switch up the mix by saying, "Now, turn to your other shoulder partner." Of course, teacher sampling must follow if there is to be any verbal feedback from students that the teacher can act on.

■ □ ■ □ ■

Elbow Partner

Again, when using the idea of partners talking to encourage and maximize feedback, "turn to your elbow partner" is often used when students are sitting at tables. This is to direct the dialogue with partners next to each other, as opposed to across from each other. This is helpful when they are sharing materials or doing lab work. Yet, to reiterate, the teacher must seek some shared responses if the feedback is to be useful for directing or redirecting the instructional flow.

Routine Teacher Expectation, Student Achievement (TESA) Techniques

Without repeating all of the research around the idea of TESA, it seems prudent to note the philosophy (Kerman, 1979) and a few of its axioms that directly relate to the idea of Routine Informative Assessments. The research on teacher expectations and the impact of student achievement posits the inextricable link between the two. When teachers have high expectations for all students, when the students believe that the teacher believes in them, student behaviors improve and achievement goes up.

The research on teacher expectations and the impact of student achievement posits the inextricable link between the two.

Several teacher behaviors that are commonly understood, yet not always promoted, are wait time, equal opportunity to respond, delving, and praise. While several have already been discussed, they appear here as well, to give testimony to the incredible impact teacher expectations have on student achievement. These are not only Routine Informative Assessment techniques that yield much data teachers can use to inform their practice, but these four strategies are also proven behaviors that foster student empowerment.

Wait Time

Wait time is a technique that requires the teacher to pause three to ten seconds following a question. It is such a simple behavior, or nonbehavior if you will, yet is so hard to actually do. It slows down the pace of the traditional classroom discussion; it changes the flow. Wait time works if teachers work it. It gives time to think to those students who are not the fastest to raise their hands, or the loudest to raise their voices.

Equal Opportunity to Respond

While this has been thoroughly exposed earlier, with tongue depressors, cards, and fishbowls, it still seems necessary to reiterate the power of this strategy when trying to maximize feedback for Routine Informative Assessment focus. When everyone talks, everyone has the privilege of learning, because the adage, "The person doing the talking is the person doing the learning," is absolutely the truth. Students must be able to say it in their own words to own it! Period!

Delving

Delve for depth. Get more information. Know that the student understands. That is what this strategy is all about. Enough said, as it has been developed earlier in this section.

Praise

Giving specific praise is what is advocated in TESA as a motivation for increased student achievement. It is mentioned here for the purpose of citation, as a Routine Informative Assessment technique. However, it is more fully developed on page 48, in reference to teacher feedback, as described and illustrated by Wiggins (2008).

Routine Vocabulary Building and Comprehension Techniques

Costa and Kallick (2000), in their book *Discovering & Exploring Habits of Mind,* address robust dispositions that include precision, accuracy, perseverance, and even creativity. These are long-term attitudes that become instilled in students as they move through a strident system of teaching, learning, and assessing. The path goes from dependent thinkers to independent problem solvers and on toward interdependence with others in collaborative endeavors.

To truly understand the habits of mind, the concepts themselves must be dissected and analyzed in order to know the many facets of meaning. That is exactly what quality teachers do as a Routine Informative Assessment technique to improve student performance. The technique is called unpacking the language and it becomes a vital skill, as students learn to assess their understanding of the expectations laid out in the standards, the assignments, and the tests.

Unpacking the Language

> **Unpacking the language is a ripe opportunity to assess student understanding of the language of standards, as well as the language of the tests.**

Unpacking the language is a ripe opportunity to assess student understanding of the language of standards, as well as the language of the tests, the assignments they do, and the tests they take. It is another Routine Informative Assessment technique that is easily woven into everyday lessons and the daily, weekly, and end-of-course tests, and, naturally, for high-stakes tests as well.

To unpack the language of the action words embedded in instructions and directions, include simple words that students do read, but it's almost a "read over." They often don't connect with the authentic meaning and thus fail to execute the task as it is presented to them.

Students typically stumble over words such as *explain, compare, analyze, outline, argue, discuss, demonstrate.* These are the words that often trip them up and consequently cause them to make mistakes, go in the wrong direction, and even lose points because of misunderstandings or misconceptions of the expectations. When teachers regularly help students "unpack the language," they become privy to the interpretation students take away from the text. It illuminates many of the problems kids face as they attempt to do their daily work.

> *Unpack the Word:* "Analyze"; first define, then apply!
>
> *Define:* To take apart, look at the parts, divide in smaller parts; find key elements.
>
> *Apply:* Analyze this statement: "Great events make great men/women!"
>
> *Great* means really super or grand, *events* means happenings and *men/women* means people. Therefore, the statement means, "Grand happenings create super people."

Now, while this seems like a ridiculous exercise in redundancy, it is necessary for many students to go through this kind of dissection in order to see the real or sometimes hidden meanings. In the end, it reveals what students are thinking and affords opportunity to redirect misguided ideas.

Tasks

Handmade Signals

Distribute three sticky notes, of three different colors, to students. Assign three signals to the colors:

Blue—Agree

Yellow—Not Sure

Pink—Disagree

■ □ ■ □ ■

Then, present a set of ten statements about the concept under study and have the students simply hold up the appropriate card to signal their response. Have them hold up blue for agreement, yellow for undecided, and pink for disagreement.

Tally the response for each, on chart paper. Debrief with a discussion that concludes with revisions for correct answers.

Then ask students to comment on what the distribution of tally marks signals about the level of student understanding in the class as a whole. Keep the conversation constructive and safe by stressing that signaling is a tool you will be using this year for routine formative assessments, which inform students and teachers alike.

Tips

Tip 1: The most important "take away" is that Routine Informative Assessments are easy to thread into the daily happenings of classroom interactions. If you are already using many of the tools and techniques listed in this discussion, keep doing them and try to do them even more frequently.

Tip 2: Also, just to push yourself, select one that is new and commit to trying it right away.

Tip 3: As a professional learning community, incorporate journals of all routine assessments regularly to use in your classrooms and to share among colleagues.

Chapter 2

Reflective Informative Assessments

Many Days—Conversations

Scenario (Reader's Theater)

Intelligent Behavior

The scene is taking place just prior to a primary level professional learning community (PLC) team meeting between two teachers, who arrived early. Mrs. Flynn is a third-grade teacher and Miss Ng teaches second grade. They are deep in conversation about a wonderful quote, recalled from the opening day ceremonies. The discussion ensues and causes significant changes in their thinking about their classroom instruction and assessment strategies.

Mrs. Flynn

Do you remember that speaker at the district meeting the first day we were back? At that presentation, the speaker said something that really struck me. He said, and I quote, because I wrote it down right here in the front of my notebook, "Intelligent behavior is knowing what to do when you don't know what to do."

Miss Ng

Oh, yes, that's right. That was Art Costa. I've heard him speak before, and I did like that comment, but I didn't think to write it down like you did. That was so smart of you!

Mrs. Flynn

Well, it really resonated with me because it's what our ultimate goal is, to have students learn to think, to problem solve, and to make sound decisions.

Miss Ng

You are right. That's exactly what we are trying to do in our professional learning community. In the PLC, we want to become more collaborative, sure. We understand that two heads are better than one. But, at the end of the day, our overriding goal is to become more reflective in our practice, for the betterment of our students.

Mrs. Flynn

I agree. It really is the same thing we want for our kids. We want them to be invested in their learning, to "own" the learning, so to speak. And one surefire way for them to do that, is for them to become more reflective about their learning.

Miss Ng

True. When kids start to be more reflective, they move into a metacognitive way of thinking. They move beyond the cognitive, or the answers per se, and into another area of reflection on how they arrived at the answers, if the answers are the best answers, and what other strategies they might have used.

Mrs. Flynn

They start thinking about their thinking and about what they call the "learning to learn" strategies. And, they look at their own learning strengths and weaknesses.

Miss Ng

It makes so much sense. It's when kids start becoming acutely aware of what they know and what they don't know.

Mrs. Flynn

And it goes back to that original statement, about intelligent behavior, " . . . knowing what to do, when you don't know what to do."

Miss Ng

It reminds me of something I saw in my homeland newspaper. In Singapore, the leaders wrote, "The goal is to educate our children so they can learn without being taught."

■ □ ■ □ ■

Mrs. Flynn

Wow! I love that! It's all about reflective thinking. Thinking about how one learns.

Miss Ng

It's reflecting on the *whys* and *hows*, as well as knowing the *whats*. It's about being aware of the process, when the process becomes the content, if you will.

Mrs. Flynn

That's so true. And it's about being a lifelong learner.

Miss Ng

Yes! Learning for a lifetime, not for a test.

Mrs. Flynn

I believe we have some important things to think about, as we consider how we might structure our classroom instruction with more focus on this idea of more explicit reflection.

Miss Ng

As I see it, it's part of a continuum. We are routinely incorporating formative assessments that cause self-appraisal. We are trying to maximize student feedback with signaling techniques, and various data gathering instruments. Now we just have to move along the continuum, by adding explicit opportunities for self-reflection.

Mrs. Flynn

That sounds good, and it sounds like it might be fairly easy to do, even though it needs to be done with some sort of planning. After all, we do want to implement reflective assessments in true and authentic ways.

Miss Ng

Yes, we will need to gather ideas about the reflection tools and techniques we use effectively already, and then find some new ones to add to the list.

■ □ ■ □ ■

Mrs. Flynn

Hey! Let's talk to the PLC members about reflective assessments. This sounds as if it might be a great professional topic for our team to pursue, if they are willing to get on board.

Miss Ng

You know, I think they will embrace reflective assessment as a way to foster ongoing productive problem solving and sound decision making for our kids. How could they not want to instill "intelligent behavior," such as reflective self-evaluation?

Mrs. Flynn

Let's go for it! See what they say.

Teachings

Defining Reflective Informative Assessments

To define the concept of Reflective Informative Assessments, the focus turns to reflection as one of the most powerful learning modes. Reflection breeds awareness and self-awareness. It breeds control over one's learning. Reflection is metacognitive by nature. It forces the teacher and the learners to step beyond the cognitive responses, outside the frame, to look in on the action and the activity. It's a momentary freeze frame that affords opportunity to think *about* reflection. In the context of classroom instruction, this means taking time to think about how one is thinking. It's about focusing on how to learn, as well as what to learn. In brief, Reflective Informative Assessments require intentional attention to the *hows* and *whys* of the teaching and learning equation. While Reflective Informative Assessments may not be used all day, every day, for time management reasons, they are integrated into the classroom interaction when quality instruction is the target. Reflective Informative

Assessments occur on *many days* throughout the classroom learning cycle.

Reflection breeds awareness and self-awareness.

Yes, reflection takes time, and it is frequently seen as an add-on to the content-focused lesson, yet the reflective moment yields so much valuable feedback data that it is becoming a critical and integral part of the lesson format. Teachers who are tuned into student achievement through student empowerment consistently embrace reflective tools and techniques. They have seen the astonishing results that occur when kids own their own learning by looking at their strengths and weaknesses, the *whys* and *wherefores* of their successes and failures and the revealing insights about another set of skills, called "learning to learn" skills.

At the end of the day, Reflective Informative Assessments are to be interpreted as the regular, consistent, and frequent "activities undertaken by the teachers and/or by their students, which provide information to be used as feedback to modify the teaching and learning activities in which they are engaged" (Black & Wiliam, 1998).

In sum, the key to understanding the category of Reflective Informative Assessment is a serious consideration of the word *reflective*. The thought is that assessments in this category are reflectively chosen and that their use results in feedback that teachers and students can subsequently reflect on when choosing the next step in learning.

Unlike Routine Informative Assessments, which occur every day, Reflective Informative Assessments occur many days, but not all. At key instruction junctures, teachers reflect on various assessment options available to them and reflectively choose the best option, given a thoughtful consideration of their students and the learning objectives they are trying to meet.

Describing

Reflective Informative Assessments have their roots in other reflective activities that have always occurred in the classroom setting. Typically, teachers have used reflective strategies as part of the normal course of subject matter lessons and assignments. Among the reflective activities in which teachers normally engage are such instructional arenas as lab logs, literary journals, independent reading choices, student portfolios and work folders, projects, and performances. These are areas that lend themselves to reflective dialogues and written thoughts and notations.

Students record in the science logs, yet they also write about their process. They often are expected to keep literary journals or reading response journals as a place to reflect on their reading. In turn, the student portfolio process usually requires three fundamental phases: collecting, selecting, and reflecting on the selected pieces. This may be the process used with work folders too. Finally, substantive projects and major performances are frequently accompanied with a reflective piece, be it a dialogue, a discussion, or in a written format. In any case, reflection is already deeply encased in classroom behaviors.

Examples of Reflective Informative Assessments

Thus, as illustrated in the previous discussion, Reflective Informative Assessments are nothing new. Yet it seems imperative to also include some relevant examples that are specific to the overall classroom assessment process, in the traditional sense of an assessment plan. Among the most obvious Reflective Informative Assessments used to inform teachers and students is to arrange these assessments into three categories: reflective learning tools called advanced organizers and note-taking foldables, reflective whole group interactions that require self-assessing behaviors, and metacognitive prompts that cue student thinking— about their own thinking and learning.

In addition, a subsequent section delineates three Reflective Informative Assessment techniques. These include reflective questioning techniques, reflective teacher feedback techniques (as opposed to the earlier discussed issue of maximizing student feedback), and reflective collaborative learning techniques.

Sensing the value of repetition, repeating an earlier discussion seems prudent at this point. In the next several sections of the chapter, titled Tools, Techniques, Tasks, and Tips, this set of reflective kinds of assessments will be delineated more fully. Each is explained comprehensively, examples are drawn, an activity for immediate use is included, and tips are given to clarify the implementation processes. Of course, the goal is to motivate practical application of these vital assessment ideas to improve classroom practices.

For clarification, the distinction made between tools and techniques is a deliberate one. *Tools* are often (though not always) objects and manipulatives, specific instruments that can be used in the classroom for immediate and relevant student feedback. They are often reusable and become part and parcel of the daily instructional methodology.

On the other hand, *techniques* comprise more intricate tactics and strategies. Reflective Informative Assessment techniques are often customized and tailored to the specific teaching and learning situation. Techniques may vary in their targeted use by complexity, intensity, and duration, depending on the particular instructional circumstance.

The *tasks* are selected to demonstrate an immediate application, while the *tips* assist with the *whys* and *wherefores* of actual implementation in K–12 classrooms. In the end, these last sections of the chapter are intended to lead the reader to clearer understandings by illustrations of actual applications.

Tools

Advanced Organizers and Note-Taking Foldables

This section focuses on the area of advanced organizers and note-taking foldables. It details the *whys* and *wherefores* of these highly motivating and brain-compatible learning, Reflective Informative Assessment tools. Included in this discussion are student journals; little pocket-size books; magic books that flip from sectioned pages to a large picture-perfect page; folded, seamless, watertight containers made famous by the Boy Scouts; *Ideas to Go!* foldable, with take-away windows; step books or ladder books; and student portfolios that feature an interlocking mechanism. Each will be presented in ways that facilitate immediate transfer and application to the K–12 classroom assessment plan.

Student Journals

The use of classroom journals is not a new idea. Teachers often expect students to journal, and traditionally, even provide the time and directions for students to execute the journaling task quite readily. Unlike some of those typical applications of journaling, Reflective Informative Assessment journals emphasize looking back or looking over the work that has been done and determining what is valued in the learning process.

To that end, students are encouraged to self-assess, peer assess, and group assess as they track their learning. The purpose of the Reflective Informative Assessment journals is to provide clear and helpful student feedback that will inform both students and teachers of the next steps needed. The journals are ongoing instruments used in the classroom quite often.

■□■□■

With that in mind, there are numerous genres that manifest the Reflective Informative Assessment journals that teachers can employ throughout the term. These include double-entry journals, dialogue journals, action journals, art journals, "on a scale of one to ten" journals, letter journals, lead-in journals, math journals, and science logs. Brief descriptions follow for each of these.

Double-Entry Journals

Double-entry journals afford two opportunities to record thoughts. The initial entry calls for a narrative description of the activity or interaction. The second entry consists of a reflection on the preceding work.

Example:

> *Description: I did some research on the Internet for my science project on a genetic disease. I chose a mental illness called bipolar disease. It's an emotional disorder that manifests itself in mood swings from depression to euphoria.*
>
> *Reflection: As I look back on what I was reading on bipolar disease, it made me think about normal mood changes that we all have. I wonder what makes it a disease, if we all have these mood swings.*

Dialogue Journals

Dialogue journals create a dialogue between two people. The dialogue can occur between a student and a teacher, with two classmates, or even between students from different classrooms. One student begins the dialogue in his or her journal and passes the journal to the other person. After writing in it, the second person returns the dialogue journal to its owner. The back and forth continues as long as the two parties are engaged and responding.

Example:

Person 1: I am frustrated with my math homework because I am confused as soon as I step away from the classroom. The teacher makes it so clear, I think I have it, but when I go to do it, I don't have it!!!!

Person 2: If you want to go over our notes before you do your homework, I would be glad to do that with you (at school, at home, or on the phone).

Action Journals

Action journals are designed to plan next steps to take. They are specifically aimed at strategic planning and appropriate next tactics. Action journals can even become contracts of sorts, in which the students present their action steps to the teacher or to a peer for consensus and approval.

Example:

The next step for my PowerPoint presentation is to select or design a background and lay out a first draft of critical slides.

"On a Scale of One to Ten" Journals

"On a scale of one to ten" journals force the student to self-evaluate with a rating. This journal has a predictable structure that is easy to use once students become familiar with it. It really makes them think about how well they understand something and determine if they think they have mastered the skill or concept. Surprisingly, kids seem to like the rating process involved.

Example:

On a scale of one to ten, I rate myself a five on the science concept of gravity. I am getting it, but I have a ways to go before I could actually explain it to someone else. I do know that gravity is what keeps us "grounded," and it's what they don't have in spaceships.

Letter Journals

Letter journals are just that: They are notes in the form of letters to someone in particular. They might be letters to the teacher, a peer, a parent, or a far-away friend. The idea behind the letter journal is to change the journaling and make it an entirely new approach. The letter journal idea came from a book by Jonathan Kozol (2007). It is called *Letters to a Young Teacher,* and he writes about teaching in this letter format. It is quite impressive.

Example:

> *Dear Ms. Stillwater,*
> *I am writing you this letter to tell you about our social studies class project. We are all "Poll Plotters" for the Presidential election. That means that each team must track a particular poll and graph it every week to see the trend lines. It is really a neat project, and I am watching the Gallop Poll. It is very official, as you know. I will keep you posted on our results.*

Lead-In Journals

Lead-in journals literally have a lead-in statement or a stem statement to prompt the students to write. These lead-ins might be provided as an ongoing list to select from or as a daily surprise from the teacher. In either case, the lead-ins provide a needed stimulus that seems to motivate the writing.

Example:

> *I wonder . . . why the author placed the setting in Africa. It seems so distant from us as teenagers in the United States of America. Even though I can relate in some ways to the boy's fear, I have never seen an animal like that in the wild, let alone be attacked by one.*

Other possible stems or lead-ins include the following:

A problem I'm having . . .

Compared to . . .

An analogy might be . . .

It's amazing that . . .

I can't explain . . .

Math Journal

The math journal has been around for some time and is currently used in some classrooms. It is a journal used to reflect on the math lesson, the problems themselves, or to think through strategies and about the best approaches to math. Teachers also might ask students to reflect on how they actually learn math best, so the students become more aware of their learning processes.

Example:

> *Working with the Pythagorean theorem in class today got me really excited. We talked about all the applications of this theory in real world terms . . . using it in the construction of buildings, bridges and boats. It gives meaning to all this math I am learning, and I like that.*

Science Log

Probably one of the first reflective tools used regularly in the classroom, the science log (or lab log) is used for observations about lab experiments. Typically, students log their data in these log books and record their findings. However, some teachers require a reflection to go along with the observation data.

Probably one of the first reflective tools used regularly in the classroom, the science log, or lab log, is used for observations about lab experiments.

Example:

The data on the pendulum swings noted above was an interesting experiment to do. It was compelling to watch the pendulum swing shorten and shorten and shorten . . . it reminded me of a song . . ."The pendulum swings . . ." I think it was a Beatles song, but I'm going to look it up tonight.

■ □ ■ □ ■

Pocket-Size Book

The pocket-size book is also called the tiny transfer book or just the little book, and it is the "best of the best," in terms of advance organizers and note-taking foldables. It is easy to make, easy to apply, and easy to tote from place to place. It is perhaps one of the most versatile and popular Reflective Informative Assessment tools available to the classroom teacher. (For directions on how to fold the pocket-size book, visit www.robinfogarty.com and click on the Ideas button.) There are many formatting options for these pocket-sized little books. These include the following:

> *Single page*
>
> *Double page format*
>
> *Two-to-a-page format*
>
> *Three-to-a-page format*
>
> *Reversible little book format*

Magic Book

The magic book is a foldable that allows reflection in two compatible ways: holistic and analytical. The magic is in the element of surprise that occurs when the tabs are pulled and the images flip from the analytical six windows to the holistic big picture. Directions for the magic book can be found on the Web site, www.robinfogarty.com. Go to the Ideas button on the menu. It can be used for many concepts that require the higher order thinking of synthesis (big picture) and analysis (parts).

Boy Scout Container

This foldable is a container for notes, rather than an actual note-taking device. It has been part of the Boy Scouts of America survival tools for many years. As the seamless container is made, it looks like a miniature Chinese take-out box. In fact, it actually holds water and is used by the Boy Scouts as a drinking cup. In the classroom, however, the Boy Scout container is used for vocabulary words, math facts, and science terms.

Take-Away Window

The take-away window is a simple fold-over, used to gather strategies. On the cover, the title is *Ideas to Go!* The inside double page is framed and titled *Take-Away Window.* All the "take-aways" are listed inside that window. It makes an effective tool to delineate the ideas that are intended for transfer and application.

Step Book

The ladder book, the step book, and the flip book are all names for this foldable. It provides various steps for note taking and is especially handy for listings, options, and choices that occur in some contexts.

Example: Students might use this advanced organizer to list the phases of the scientific method:

Ask a question

Do background research

Construct a hypothesis

Test your hypothesis by doing an experiment

Analyze your data and draw a conclusion

Communicate your results

Student Portfolios

Student portfolios are highly effective assessment tools that, by their very nature, foster reflective learning. The key steps involve creating a folder to hold student work and then including the processes of collection, selection, and reflection. That means collecting various pieces in a working portfolio, selecting several for a showcase portfolio, and finally reflecting on the final selections. These can be used for a unit of work, an entire term, or for intermittent work throughout one subject area.

> **Student portfolios are highly effective assessment tools that, by their very nature, foster reflective learning.**

Whole Group Assessment-Driven Reflections

The marvelous genius behind the whole group reflective assessments tools is in their public format. Each student is basically involved in a "forced response" strategy by being required to take a stand on an imaginary graphed line or axis. In the process of deciding where to stand, each student must reflect on the idea and choose a spot on the imaginary graph line.

Agree/Disagree Anticipation Guide

The agree/disagree anticipation guide is composed of a set of statements framed around a concept. Students read and respond to the statements by reflecting on whether or not they agree with the statement. Once they have reflected and responded, they dialogue with a partner, thus fostering further reflection.

Example: Agree/Disagree: Drug and Alcohol Unit of Study

1. A glass of beer and a glass of wine have the same amount of alcohol content.

2. The drinking age is a national decision and law.

3. Alcohol is a legal drug.

4. MADD stands for Men Against Dirty Drugs.

People Search

The people search is an interactive reflective tool that causes students to "find someone who . . ." will respond to a statement. By moving about the group, students have reflective dialogues with a number of students. It gives them a chance to reflect on different points of view, as they examine their own thoughts on the issues.

Example: People Search: Global Warming

Find someone who . . .

1. Agrees that global warming is manmade and tells you why.

2. Compares global warming: Global warming is like _____ because both _____.

3. Ranks the country that causes the most global warming the same as you:

   ___ USA ___ China ___ Venezuela ___ Saudi Arabia ___ Russia

4. Believes carbon emissions from jets cause more pollution than car emissions, and so forth.

Human Graph

The human graph asks students to reflect on a statement and literally take a stand in a graph-like format. Once the student has chosen a spot on the graph, that student is expected to share the reason behind the stand. Thus, the student not only reflects on an idea, but also has the opportunity to consider the other points of view that are voiced.

Example:

> *Quality education is an American right.*
> *Strongly Agree / Agree / Not Sure / Disagree / Strongly Disagree*

Metacognitive Prompts

Metacognitive prompts are simply questions that cue students to reflect on their own learning. Metacognition is often defined as thinking about thinking or learning about how to learn. These types of questions often focus on the *why* and *how* of something, as opposed to the *what, when,* and *where.* Metacognitive or reflective questions foster student awareness and control over their own learning.

Metacognitive prompts are simply questions that cue students to reflect on their own learning.

They provide a pivot point for mindful consideration of the task, the work, or the problem solving and decision making that will occur, is occurring, or has occurred. Following this introduction, there are specific examples of metacognitive questions, including Mrs. Potter's Questions, Ms. Poindexter's Questions, a Plus, Minus, Interesting strategy, and a new take on the traffic light strategy.

Mrs. Potter's Questions

Four critical and commonly used reflective questions are manifested in a set titled Mrs. Potter's Questions. The questions invite thoughtful comments on the following perspectives:

1. What were you trying to do?

2. What went well?

3. What might you do differently next time?

4. Do you need any help?

It's easy to see how these four questions lead the student or student group to think through what they have just done. Of course, they can be asked in the future tense in anticipation of what they think will occur. In either case, they are serious and true reflections that help students examine the strengths and weaknesses of their efforts.

■☐■☐■

Ms. Poindexter's Questions

Ms. Poindexter's Questions ask students to review their recent endeavors and evaluate the process. The two questions ask the following:

1. Where did you get stuck?

2. How did you get unstuck?

In posing these two questions, the teacher is asking students to think deeply about their processes and the procedures they employed. In turn, they are expected to examine what was hard to do, and what they did to move things along. In asking for these kinds of reflections, the teacher intentionally implies that everyone gets stuck in the process of doing complex tasks, and that everyone has strategies to find alternative solutions. It becomes a highly effective informative assessment tool that students can take into many of their life situations, as well as apply to many school situations.

Plus, Minus, Interesting (PMI)

Plus, Minus, Interesting, or PMI, is a De Bono (1992) strategy that requires a look at three perspectives: the positive or the pluses, the negatives or minuses, and the neutral or the interesting.

P (Plus) means anything that seems to enhance; the benefits, the good side

M (Minus) targets anything that seems to diminish or take away from; the detriments; the bad side

I (Interesting) focuses on anything that is not really a plus or minus, but rather a connection or thought that seems neutral, yet relevant

Again, PMI implies questions of evaluation and analysis in terms of the many facets of an idea or task. PMI is a reflective tool that has multiple applications.

Traffic Light Strategy

The traffic light strategy can be used most effectively as a self-assessment tool (Black, Harrison, Lee, Marshall, & Wiliam, 2003). Using three assessment levels that simulate the traffic light (green, yellow, and red), the students label their work, green, yellow, and red, to signal their depth of understanding. When the teacher asks for a show of hands, that teacher has promoted and maximized feedback for review yet has fostered student self-awareness as well.

Green—Good, solid understanding; could tell others

Yellow—Partial, some sense of what it's about, idea is developing; need collaborations to clarify and affirm

Red—Not sure, little real understanding; could not tell others; need reinforcement

Checklists and Rubrics (Criteria in Kid-Friendly Terms)

Checklists, based on critical criteria, are reflective tools that inform both students and teachers about adherence or lack of adherence to the items delineated on the checklist.

Often, the checklist of requirements for a project or a performance is drawn from the actual wording of the standards of learning. The language is examined and then listed in the criteria. For example:

Standard: Students will be familiar with works of fiction and nonfiction.

Criteria Checklist: Persuasive essay on the presidential election

1. Completed three- to five-page essay
2. Evidence of nonfiction resources
3. Evidence of fiction resources
4. Statement of argument

5. Details supporting argument

6. Literary conventions

Once the checklist is developed, enhancing that checklist can create a scoring rubric. By establishing critical criteria (resources, mechanics, content) and by developing quality indicators (developing, competent, proficient, above and beyond), the rubric takes shape.

The rubric provides the rigor of not only a checklist of criteria, but also the specific indicators of the quality of the work. Checklists reflect whether or not the element is included, while rubrics reflect the inclusion of the key elements, as well as the quality indicators of how well the work was done. A complete scoring rubric is presented later in this chapter under Reflective Informative Assessment techniques.

Reflective Collaborative Learning

The person doing the talking is the person doing the learning! That is the philosophy that drives the constructive classroom. If students make meaning in their minds, then it follows that opportunities for cognitive rehearsal might foster deeper understanding and personal meaning. That opportunity for cognitive rehearsal is what occurs in cooperative structures. When peers dialogue, when small groups talk and share, when students reflect in consistent and continual ways through threaded discussions or blogs (Web logs) on the Internet, the reflection flourishes. Here is a set of collaborative tools that promote and produce Reflective Informative Assessments.

The person doing the talking is the person doing the learning!

Cooperative Learning Roles and Responsibilities

Cooperative groups respond to structures that guide the work of the group. One way, frequently used to ensure the participation of all members of the group, is the assignment of roles and responsibilities. The roles are determined by the task at hand. Typically, the roles and responsibilities might include the following:

Materials manager—Gets any materials or supplies needed for the task

Recorder—Does the recording on larger poster paper for all to review

Reporter—Does the speaking for the group when reporting out is needed

Encourager—Offers encouraging words (good job, way to go) and signals (A-OK, thumbs up)

Traveler—Moves about the room and gathers ideas from other groups

Interestingly, the roles are sometimes changed depending on the subject matter context, as well as by the nature of the task.

For example, if the context is math class, the roles might be as follows:

Inventory controller—Gets supplies

Calculator—Does the computation on the calculator

Trouble shooter—Researches and investigates problem areas

Statistician—Gathers and analyzes data

A science class might use the following roles:

Investigator—Task leader

Technician—Lab responsibilities

Logger—Logs all observation and data

Scientific writer—Prepares written report

While roles are not always explicit in collaborative work, it seems prudent to utilize this strategy in order to include all members in the endeavor. With full participation, real reflection in the entire process is more likely to happen and more likely to yield rich and relevant feedback from the participants.

Peer Tutors

> **The concept of using peer tutors is a powerful teaching and learning tool that dictates dialogue, conversation, and reflective observations.**

The concept of using peer tutors is a powerful teaching and learning tool that dictates dialogue, conversation, and reflective observations. When peers tutor each other or when one peer is assigned to tutor another peer, the dynamics are conducive to reflective learning opportunities. For example, when a peer tutors another in math, that tutor is likely to ask mindful questions that might sound like these:

"What do you think you need to do next?"

"Why did you do that?"

"Are you expecting a larger number or a smaller number?"

"Do you need help with that part?"

Notice that the questions are quite reflective in nature and easily foster a thoughtful response by the peer being tutored. Peer tutors also have this kind of reflective dialogue as an integral part of their ongoing conversations. Peer tutors offer a viable and useful tool for classrooms focused on informative assessments.

Cooperative Learning Tear Share

The Cooperative Learning Tear Share is a specific tool that fosters teamwork and reflective summaries around a reading, viewing, or another input piece of some kind. This is how this reflective tool works: A selected article or reading is the centerpiece of the activity. The groups are arranged with four participants, seated on four chairs facing each other like the points of a compass. Participants number off, one, two, three, and four.

They are then given the four questions related to the article, and they write them on a paper folded into four numbered sections. Everyone reads the article, and everyone responds to the four questions. Once they have all completed the responses, they tear the papers into four sections and pass each numbered section to the person designated that number. One's go to the number one person, two's to the two, and so on.

The final piece involves each member reviewing the four comments for that question and preparing an oral summary for the team. Once everyone is ready, the sharing round begins. Each person shares the responses in a reflective summary statement. Discussion follows after all four have given their summaries.

This is a highly effective strategy that is active, engaging, and involving. For the cooperative strategy to work, every person must become an invested member of the team. In turn, the team reflection on the responses is a natural outcome of this powerful cooperative structure.

Blogs

The idea of creating classroom or team Web logs or blogs to encourage Reflective Informative Assessments is something students embrace quite readily. It is the technology format that many of them are so comfortable with and use on a regular basis. This Reflective Informative Assessment tool lends itself to continual and consistent inputs from students. It's kind of an anytime, anywhere tool that can have real impact as it takes root in classroom

> **The idea of creating classroom or team Web logs or blogs to encourage Reflective Informative Assessments is something students embrace quite readily.**

reflective assessment strategies that inform and influence the teaching and learning. For teachers who are unsure of how to implement this tool, simply ask your information technology people or ask the kids. There is always someone in the classroom that is techno-savvy enough to get the blogging underway.

Techniques

Reflective Questioning Techniques

When teachers spend more time planning instruction than grading papers, they are showing a shift from "quality control to quality assurance," according to Dylan Wiliam (2007). The quality control is when grades record the quality turned in, whereas "quality assurance" is when the teacher monitors and adjusts instruction based on intentional and deliberate informative assessments methodologies.

Range-Finding Questions

Some of the most current assessment writings reference the use of "range-finding questions." While the term may be new, the concept really is not. Range-finding questions are simply questions posed before instruction, to find out the range of the students' prior knowledge.

> **Range-finding questions are simply questions posed before instruction, to find out the range of the students' prior knowledge.**

Though this is a simple concept in theory, it is often not used consistently. All teachers have faced a moment, about fifteen to twenty minutes into instruction on a new topic, when they realize that the students have absolutely no idea what they are talking about. The students lacked the necessary prior knowledge.

Indeed, it takes time to develop and pose appropriate range-finding questions, but even more time is saved. If a class of thirty students spends ineffective time going down an inappropriate instruction path for 15 minutes, 450 minutes of collective instructional time is lost. Teachers who effectively use Routine Informative Assessment tools to find the range of their students' prior knowledge are steered away from inappropriate instructional paths. Time in their class is used consistently, in the most effective manner.

Hinge-Point Questions

While teachers continually present portions of content and then "check for understanding," Leahy, Lyon, Thompson, and Wiliam (2005) make that cycle more thoughtful by specifically naming and discussing the lesson's "hinge point." It is called a hinge point because, "the lesson can go in different directions depending on student responses" (p. 21).

> **It is called a hinge point because, "the lesson can go in different directions depending on student responses."**

If the responses to hinge-point questions are consistently correct, the teacher moves the class along to the next instruction topic or to independent practice. If the responses are consistently incorrect, reteaching is warranted. If responses are mixed, then the teacher must decide what sort of quick "clean up" activities are needed. With any turn of the hinge, teachers' practices and instructional decisions are informed if they are using Routine Informative Assessments.

Perhaps the most difficult turn of the hinge to manage is when student responses are mixed. At this point, the teacher has a unique opportunity to involve students in peer instruction. If, through Routine Informative Assessment strategies that maximize feedback, the teacher can judge that at least 50% of the students in the class know the correct response, peer instruction will likely be highly effective. There are enough students in the class that understand the concept. Through peer instruction, these students can then help their classmates.

When peer instruction is used in this informed manner, everyone benefits. The students who grasp the content at the hinge point will gain deeper understanding through explaining the content in their own words to their peers. Their peers who were struggling at the hinge point will be brought up to speed. Additionally, many teachers report that in these instances, peer instruction is far superior to anything they might have offered in reteaching because, when teaching their peers, students translate the content into more kid-friendly terms.

Reflective Questions (Metacognition)

Reflective questions are highly effective when seeking insight and mindfulness about student learning. These

---
Reflective questions are highly effective when seeking insight and mindfulness about student learning.

---

questions ask students to think about their thinking, to learn about their learning. These questions ask students to step back from the action and look in on their own thinking and behaviors. Metacognitive questions often look at strengths and weaknesses, what was easy and what was hard, as well as feelings and emotional reactions to the situation. As mentioned earlier, these questions question the *hows* and *whys* of the moment, rather than the *whats* and *wherefores*.

A fifth-grade teacher posed an example of a rich and robust metacognitive question during her math class. Early in the term, she asked them to respond to this question by taking a stand on an imaginary graph: How much do you know about *how* you learn math? Take a stand on one of the five points: (1) a lot, (2) a little, (3) not sure, (4) not much, (5) next to nothing.

To reflect on this metacognitive question, about what they knew about how they learn, the teacher placed the focus on informative reflective assessments, rather than on actual math performance results. It was an explicit approach to reflect on the learning process. It was a moment in the instructional scenario that asked students to be thoughtful about their learning processes.

The teacher revisited this later in the term, and to the surprise of the students, their awareness, understanding and control over their own learning had changed quite dramatically. They noted that they had become much better at thinking about their learning modes and adjusting, revising, and revamping old habits that often had caused carelessness and inaccuracies in their math work. It is this kind of reflection that informs classroom practices.

Reflective Teacher Feedback Techniques

Feedback is the breakfast of champions. Feedback is what gives them grains of truth to act upon on the next round. Feedback is what allows champions to refine their skills to the finest edge. It is the pointed comment, the relevant coaching, and the fine-tuned advice that translates into a better, improved, more skillful performance. When feedback is descriptive, timely, relevant, and constructive, the learner welcomes it. When it is obscure, long removed from the actual occurrence, irrelevant and highly critical, feedback is lost on the learner.

Feedback is the breakfast of champions.

In the following discussion, several types of feedback techniques are presented. When used appropriately, these feedback techniques inform the learner in reflective ways that can be acted upon. These techniques include descriptive feedback, focused marking, use of benchmarked papers, peer assessments, such as peer editing, and rubric development.

Descriptive Feedback

The secret to feedback is in giving actionable feedback, feedback that is descriptive in nature and illuminates strengths and weaknesses. In trying to illustrate this concept of descriptive feedback, the reference is Wiggins (2008). He discusses feedback with some telling points about what it isn't and what it is.

Feedback—What it is not: Feedback is not praise. It is not an evaluation. It is not a number on a standardized test.

Feedback—What it is not: Feedback is not praise. It is not an evaluation. It is not a number on a standardized test. Feedback is not "Good job." It is not "B." Feedback is not "I'm disappointed in your essay." It is not "Approaching mastery."

Feedback—What it is: Feedback is useful information about performance. It is actionable information that empowers students.

Feedback—What it is: Feedback is useful information about performance. It is critical to effective learning. It is value-neutral help on various assignments and tasks. It is actionable information that empowers students to make the needed adjustments. Feedback is, "Joan, you can do two column multiplication, but you often make avoidable errors, because you are skipping a critical step in your reasoning." It is, "The title to your narrative is telling and inviting. You might want to weave it into your story." Feedback is, "José, you might eliminate many careless errors if you take the time to use the 'check for accuracy' strategy we practiced."

In addition to feedback providing the needed cues for improvement, many times the feedback comes from the activity itself. Students often notice some quirk in the problem or the solution and realize that "something is not right." This internal feedback leads to reexamination and readjustments. For example, in sports, the athlete often adjusts his swing of the golf club or her grip on the tennis racket, simply based on the previous results. This is the authentic feedback loop that is the desired method. Yet teachers often must provide the feedback, until the automatic feedback loop becomes obvious to the student.

■ □ ■ □ ■

Use of Benchmark Papers

The use of benchmarked papers can be a powerful Reflective Informative Assessment technique that provides valuable information for teachers and students. A quick story illustrates the essence of this idea. After receiving only one exemplary score (+4) for the "constructed response question" on the fourth-grade state assessment test, one principal was eager to understand what other "+4 Exemplary" responses looked like. Exactly what was the key to receiving a benchmarked paper that received a score of "+4"?

To satisfy her curiosity, she e-mailed all other elementary buildings in the district and asked her colleagues to send her copies of any papers that had received a "+4" rating on the same constructed response question. Long story short, she and her fourth-grade teachers examined and analyzed the critical elements of ten "+4 Exemplary" responses and subsequently, developed a scoring rubric of criteria and quality indicators. They were now ready to change their instruction in ways that would prepare students for striking improvements in construction responses.

In this Reflective Informative Assessment strategy, teachers take the time and make the effort to educate students about the critical differences between quality work and deficient work. They may begin by showing a high quality paper and walking students through an analysis about the components that make it a "star" paper. From that process, students may form a rubric of the key criteria and then actually discern quality descriptive indicator statements. Then the teacher may hand out several papers that represent the various levels of quality and ask students to rate them using the rubric. They may work in pairs or teams to do this. Only after they have explored this scoring process are they given the task to actually do the paper. Now they are informed learners, and this information will impact their work quite dramatically.

Samples of benchmarked papers can be found on various state test Web sites. One in particular, Delaware, is cited here to give the reader a quick reference. These samples will quickly illustrate the gradient differences evidenced in the samples. This is relevant information that is revealed when professionals use this Reflective Informative Assessment technique and eventually share with students.

Peer Assessment

One of the most appropriate and appealing Reflective Informative Assessment techniques is in the use of peer assessments. This might be peer editing, peer coding, or even peer rating. All three of these strategies inform student performance in helpful ways.

Peer editing is a common practice that requires a set of criteria the peer targets.

Peer editing is a common practice that requires a set of criteria the peer targets. This might be grammar and spelling; paragraphing; complex sentences; logical organization; well-stated, beginning, middle, and ending format; or simply what was a strength of the paper and what was a weakness.

Peer coding is a more sophisticated informative assessment technique that calls for a perusal of the work. As peers review the work, they code various elements that have been previously established. For example, the peer reviewers of an essay might have two simple codes: 1 for thesis statement and 2 for supporting details. Thus, as they review, they are looking specifically for these two components and are coding 1 and 2 throughout the piece.

Peer rating is a third peer assessment technique that is reflective by nature. Students are instructed to "rate" each other's work on a scale of one to ten. They must provide written justification for the rating. The final step is a peer dialogue about the rating. This conversation provides fertile ground for shared opinions and personal insights.

Rubric Development: Rubric standard, criteria, indicators

A scoring rubric is a guide that provides a clear and useful framework for fruitful feedback, which can be used to improve performance. Using a checklist of criteria established in the standard or benchmark, a scoring rubric with quality indicators is a logical next step (Burke, 2004). To develop the scoring rubric from the checklist, the criteria are consolidated and quality indicators are developed along a continuum. Table 2.1 is a quick example of what this process yields, in terms of a scoring rubric for assessing and informing the student and the teacher about the quality of the product or performance.

> **A scoring rubric is a guide that provides a clear and useful framework for fruitful feedback.**

Peer assessments tend to provide highly candid feedback that is often "right on point." Interestingly, peer assessments carry a special respect and acceptance by the students. They are eager to see what their peers think about their work and usually respond quite positively to this assessment technique.

When teachers codevelop the checklist and rubrics with students, the student reflections are even more meaningful, as the students have a deeper understanding of the elements. Thus, the information that can be gleaned from the checklist and rubric criteria and indicators can be extremely relevant.

Comments That Reference Criteria Instead of Grades

Instead of simply grading student work, the teacher might give comments that reference criteria. For example, by saying, "There are ___ wrong. Find which ones," the teacher shifts the focus from a point-in-time mark, to a corrective process. Students are now charged with the task of checking their math for accuracy, which is the very skill the teacher might be stressing with math computation.

Table 2.1 Persuasive Essay: Scoring Rubric

	Developing	*Competent*	*Proficient*	*Above/Beyond*
Research *Evidence of fiction and nonfiction resources*	Little evidence of fiction and nonfiction references	Sufficient evidence of fiction and nonfiction references	Much evidence of fiction and nonfiction references	Overwhelming evidence of fiction and nonfiction references
Content *Logical development of persuasive argument*	Attempt to develop persuasive argument	Logical development of persuasive argument	Reasoned and robust development of persuasive argument	Insightful and rigorous development of persuasive argument
Conventions *Grammar, spelling, punctuation, syntax*	Some misuse of conventions	Appropriate use of conventions	Notable use of conventions to carry the argument	Exceptional use of conventions that lend impact to the argument

Another example might be the comment, "There were five required paragraphs, each with a particular focus: (1) opening statement, (2) detail 1, (3) detail 2, (4) detail 3, (5) closing. Check with a partner to see if you have met the criteria." Again, the focus shifts to reflective assessments rather than simply a letter or numerical rating.

Reflective Collaborative Learning Techniques

One final Reflective Informative Assessment technique involves collaboration, as well as all of the benefits that go with those strategies. "Two heads are better than one!" is a known and accepted fact. There is a synergy that happens when people put their heads together. The result is more than the sum of its parts. In this last Reflective Informative Assessment technique, there are two ideas presented: interactive face-to-face conversations and interactive remote conversations.

Interactive Face-to-Face Conversations

Within the section on face-to-face classroom interactions, there are four types that seem significant: teacher to student, student to teacher, student to student, and hypothetically, student to self.

Teacher-to-Student Interactions

Teacher-to-student interactions are commonplace. When one looks in on a classroom and asks the question, "Who's doing the talking?" the answer, more often than not, is the teacher. It is common practice for the teacher to lead the discussion, direct the questioning, and summarize student responses. These are critical interactions that set the tenor and pace of classroom instruction.

When one looks in on a classroom and asks the question, "Who's doing the talking?" the answer, more often than not, is the teacher.

Student-to-Teacher Interactions

Student-to-teacher interactions are coveted interactions in the classroom. Teachers want students to respond, to react, and to interact to classroom input. Teachers use many structures to encourage this student-to-teacher interaction. They may call on a particular student, address the entire class with rhetorical questions, or sample several student responses in an effort to get more involvement.

Student-to-teacher interactions are coveted interactions in the classroom.

Student-to-Student Interactions

Relevant and meaningful student-to-student interactions are highly sought after by teachers in quality classrooms. They understand that this is how students learn to work using skillful teamwork, to seek team consensus, and to celebrate team accomplishments. Student-to-student interaction most often occurs in partner or small group work, when peers are talking and discussing the tasks at hand. Sometimes, however, student-to-student interactions happen when one or a group of students are presenting to other students. In either case, student-to-student interactions occur when the students are involved and invested in the team effort.

Student-to-Self Interactions

Student-to-self interactions are manifested by an internal voice of the student himself, reflecting, reacting, revising, revisiting, and reframing. This is the "metacognitive moment" that the student owns. It is this internal Reflective Informative Assessment that teachers strive to develop and refine. This is how students become more self-aware, self-monitoring, and self-assessing. It is the ultimate reflective assessment that informs performance.

> **Student-to-self interactions are manifested by an internal voice of the student himself.**

Interactive Remote Conversations (E-Mail Buddies)

E-mail buddies work well as a way to continue the classroom interactions. The e-mail buddies can be assigned by project, for a group, or for the term. When they are e-mail buddies working on the same project, the students' e-mail conversations center on the project tasks. When they are e-mail buddies in the same group, they e-mail about assignments or concerns for the group. And, when they are e-mail buddies assigned for the term, their e-mailing covers more comprehensive interactions. These may range from sharing information on homework assignments to comparing strategies for completing their term paper.

Regardless of the exact nature of the e-mail buddies as designed by the teacher, the idea of extending interactions beyond the classroom walls has a powerful effect. Students naturally move into Reflective Informative Assessments as these informal conversations unfold.

Tasks

Reflective Informative Assessments provide a needed texture to the classroom interactions. They move the cognitive focus to a metacognitive or learning-to-learn focus, in which the students are privy to examination of their own thinking and actions. One activity that guides this critical process is found in the metacognitive questions that students can ask themselves and their group members.

The Reflective Informative Assessment task presented here provides a set of explicitly reflective questions that students can easily embrace. The tool used in this activity is called an accordion book. It is a foldable that is made by folding a strip of paper back and forth to create an accordion effect. On each of the eight pages, students gather a metacognitive reflection tool, in the form of cuing questions. These are the eight reflective tools that inform students and teachers about the learning process. They help reveal what's working and what's not in the classroom instructional arena.

1. Mrs. Potter's Questions

What were you trying to do?

What went well?

What might you do differently if you do this kind of thing again?

Do you need any help?

2. Mr. Parnes' Questions

How does this connect to something you already know?

How might you use this in the future?

3. Ms. Poindexter's Questions

Where did you get stuck?

How did you get unstuck?

4. Mr. Pete's Questions

Tell me more. Can you give me an example of that?

How do you feel about that?

5. Mr. De Bono's Questions

What were the pluses?

What were the minuses?

What was interesting?

6. Mr. Lickert's Scale

On a scale of one to ten, I think we were a ___ because ___.

7. Ms. Foggy's Questions

What was one highlight of the project?

What was one insight you gained from the process?

8. Mrs. Gregory's Questions

What was an "Aha!" moment you remember?

What was an "Oh, No!" moment you recall?

After students have created their reflective questions booklet, they have these to use whenever they are reflecting on a team effort or an individual assignment. These become quick-glance tools for informative reflective assessment moments structured into the interactions.

Tips

Tip 1: Make reflection a part of the instructional interaction by stepping back from the answers and looking at the processes.

Tip 2: Use specific tools that foster reflection to be sure it is not overlooked. It's easy to just move right along with classroom interactions at a rapid pace.

Tip 3: Don't forget about the "metacognitive moment" that is so revealing of the teaching and learning process. It is one of the key elements that put the quality classroom on the road to informative assessments, as part and parcel of the whole classroom interaction package.

Chapter 3

Rigorous Informative Assessments
Some Days — Philosophical Shift

Scenario (Reader's Theater)

Distracted Detectives

The scene takes place in a high school science department meeting. Two members are discussing the need for more analysis of the data available to them about student achievement. They are feeling the need to take apart the test questions and figure out the real reasons why kids are missing particular questions. They think that this might be a key to what's behind the drop in test scores on the ninth-grade tests.

Mr. Hauwai

You know, I've been thinking about those ninth-grade test scores. I'm still trying to figure out why the scores are down. It's really quite a drop from last year's group.

Mrs. Trumbull

Yeah! I'm with you. It's down by 25%. That's a lot. It's not clear to me what's going on.

Mr. Hauwai

It's kind of a conundrum to me. The kids are so motivated in the science classes. They love the labs. And even though they don't always read the text, between the lectures and the labs, it seems they have opportunities to develop real understanding. It doesn't make sense that they are doing so poorly on the test questions. Something is not transferring.

Mrs. Trumbull

I agree. I wonder how we can go deeper into this issue? Maybe with some deliberate, rigorous examination of the data — some real detective work, if you will — we can figure out what we need to do differently to get these kids on board with the tests and with more authentic understandings of the science concepts.

Mr. Hauwai

I like that idea. It's kinda what's been gnawing at my brain too. I was thinking that we might need to take some time to dig a bit deeper and learn more about dissecting robust test questions, and even about writing our own good test questions to prepare students better. How do you think we should begin our investigation?

Mrs. Trumbull

Let's determine what questions were missed and take a look at the actual questions. Then we might be able to see some patterns emerge. Maybe we can also begin to understand how to discern the distracters that get the kids off track.

Mr. Hauwai

I've been reading about some schools that are doing exactly that. In fact, apparently there are ways to determine what they call "distracters" in the questions. These "distracters" confuse the issues and often take the kids in a different direction from the intended response.

Mrs. Trumbull

That shouldn't be too hard to do. We know the purpose of the questions, you know, the target concepts or skills being tested. Also, they mentioned in this same article that there is software out there for writing robust test questions of our own.

Mr. Hauwai

Absolutely! You are so right on! And what's more, we might gain some real insights into the conceptions and misconceptions that the students have taken away from our lessons. It could be a real eye-opener for us.

Mrs. Trumbull

Yes, indeed! I know this is a bit rigorous and we will need to set aside some time to actually do this investigation. Are you up for it?

Mr. Hauwai

You bet! This whole notion of the drop in test scores has me concerned. I'm ready, willing, and able to do whatever it takes to get some answers.

Mrs. Trumbull

You're on! Let's find a time in the next week or so, before we get distracted. No pun intended!

Mr. Hauwai

How about next Monday, following the department meeting? We can even mention it today and see if others might want to join us on this new venture.

The others have arrived, and the meeting is about to begin.

Teachings

Defining Rigorous Informative Assessments

In defining the concept, *Rigorous Informative Assessment,* the term *rigorous* is the operative word. Rigor is not about something being difficult or hard; rather, it involves care and commitment to persist with the rigors of the investigation; to persevere until the task is done. It calls for willingness on the part of the teacher to go above and beyond the routine duties of the classroom. It dictates allowance for "extra time" to devote to professional learning endeavors that move the team and the students forward in dramatically different ways.

> **Rigorous Informative Assessments occur with purpose and intentionality.**

Therefore, Rigorous Informative Assessments are not used routinely, all day, every day, and they may not even be used with predictable regularity. They occur on some days, special days, when time is set aside and talent has been tapped. Rigorous Informative Assessments occur with purpose and intentionality. These rigorous kinds of informative assessments require great deliberation and mindfulness.

These rigorous assessments sound like they are time and energy intensive, and there is some truth to that notion. There is real work to be done, for sure. However, once developed, the tools and techniques of Rigorous

Informative Assessments are there forever. They become a part of the assessment scene and can be used again and again.

Yet Rigorous Informative Assessments are to be interpreted as the occasional research and development "activities undertaken by the teachers and/or by their students, which provide information to be used as feedback to modify the teaching and learning activities in which they are engaged" (Black & Wiliam, 1998).

Describing Rigorous Informative Assessments

Rigorous Informative Assessments are similar to other rigorous endeavors teachers engage in, within the framework of continuous, ongoing development and revision of curriculum, instruction, and assessment. Such rigorous activities that already exist include the occasional curriculum writing projects, the intermittent development of a new report card, or the team creation of a dynamic integrated unit of study. In these types of rich and robust projects, teachers devote their time and energy to the cause. While they dedicate themselves to see the project through, tremendous professional growth often occurs as a result of these Herculean efforts.

> **Rigorous Informative Assessments are similar to other rigorous endeavors teachers engage in.**

Examples of Rigorous Informative Assessments

Examples of Rigorous Informative Assessments are abundant. The more focused teachers become on assessing for learning, the more investigative professional projects appear on the horizon.

Among the menu of options for Rigorous Informative Assessment tools, there are three distinctive categories that come to mind. They are assessment areas that require intense attention to fully develop and implement. These rigorous kinds of informative assessment tools include the creation of performance tasks and accompanying performance assessments, such as scoring rubrics; grading practices that change motivational dynamics and are more complex than current practices; and electronic test creation, with a focus on the types of questions and tests that provide the most feedback on strengths and weaknesses.

In the realm of Rigorous Informative Assessment techniques, there are also three classifications of strategies that seem helpful. These Rigorous Informative Assessment techniques include the groupings of higher order thinking, tests (test questions and test analysis), and summative assessments as informative assessments.

Again, apologies for revisiting an earlier discussion, yet it seems a relevant reminder before reading on. In the next several sections of the chapter, titled Tools, Techniques, Tasks, and Tips, this set of rigorous kinds of assessments will be delineated more fully. Each is explained comprehensively, examples are drawn, an activity for immediate use is included, and tips are given to clarify the implementation processes. Of course, the goal is to motivate practical application of these vital assessment ideas to improve classroom practices.

For clarification, the distinction made between tools and techniques is a deliberate one. *Tools* are often objects and manipulatives, specific instruments that can be used in the classroom for immediate and relevant student feedback. They are often reusable, and become part and parcel of the daily instructional methodology.

On the other hand, *techniques* comprise more intricate tactics and strategies. Rigorous Informative Assessment techniques are often customized and tailored to the specific teaching and learning situation. Techniques may vary in their targeted use by complexity, intensity, and duration, depending on the particular instructional circumstance.

The *tasks* are selected to demonstrate an immediate application, while the *tips* assist with the *whys* and *wherefores* of actual implementation in K–12 classrooms. In the end, these last sections of the chapter are intended to lead the reader to clearer understandings by illustrations of actual applications.

Tools

Performance Assessment

Performance assessment is the most authentic form of assessment. It is the "proof in the pudding," as they say. The performance itself reveals much about the learner's grasp of the information. It speaks volumes about the level of understanding and the execution of quality. The performance assessment can be formative or summative in nature, but it also can be objective or subjective. It is often more likely to be subjective, based on knowledge of substance and preferences about style of the viewer.

Performance assessment is the most authentic form of assessment.

Thus the need for the scoring rubric is born. Subjective assessment is precisely why a scoring rubric is used to measure performance. The rubric provides a tool for a more objective evaluation or appraisal. Co-developing the scoring rubric with students and utilizing that scoring rubric prior to the performance fully supports students as they actually prepare the performance.

Performance Tasks

Just a quick glance at the idea of developing authentic learning tasks that provide the opportunity for students to bring their concepts and skills to bear on a product or performance. These rich, robust, and rigorous tasks often begin by presenting a scenario to set the stage for independent or group investigations. Each scenario has two critical elements: a stakeholder role and an open-ended problem. It may also have requirements for the investigation that the teacher, the students, or both have agreed upon, as part and parcel of the completed assignment.

The stakeholder role presents a specific point that sets the stage for the investigation. For example, if students were conducting a civics investigation around the topic of appropriate legal age for alcohol use, various teams might be given different roles: the teen, the parent, or the county sheriff. In addition, the scenario is expected to be open-ended. It should not deliberately determine the direction of the work in any way.

The stakeholder role presents a specific point that sets the stage for the investigation.

Finally, there might be required elements to demonstrate the path of the investigation. For example, the requirements might ask for evidence of any or all of the following: Internet research, a map, a journal, a timeline, a persuasive essay, an electronic presentation, an interview, a graphic organizer, a fiction and nonfiction source, a primary source, a three-dimensional artifact, and so forth.

Here are some samples of simple "performance tasks" that often begin with the stakeholder role, "You are . . . ," and leave the problem open-ended. There may also be a section that begins, "You will . . . ," to delineate the requirements of the investigation.

Scenario 1: Senator for a Day

You are a senator from one of the original thirteen colonies and you are preparing to address the entire Senate with your honored opinion, advocating secession from the Union. You will provide a map of the United States, an outline of

your speech, a list of resources, historical quotes, a period costume, and a persuasive essay in the form of an elegant speech that is videotaped. How will you proceed?

Scenario 2: Civil War Sites

You are a travel agent and have been asked to design a tour of Civil War, Revolutionary War, and Westward Movement sites. You will provide a map of the area, a promotional brochure, a description of each site and a listing of your selected sites with written justification for the selections. What will you do to complete this task?

Scenario 3: Grammar Police

You are a member of the grammar police. You must be able to identify the grammar violation, cite the rules that govern the proper language, and issue citations accordingly. You will provide a grammar guide, a list of rules and consequences, a ticket booklet, and a plan for implementing the new classroom regulations.

Scenario 4: Space Station

You are an astronaut and have been appointed to the team designated to open and operate the new space station satellite. You will provide a historical reference paper, scientific data, pictures of other space explorations, goals for the mission, a list of supplies needed by the astronauts, a timeline for the launch, a newspaper headline, and an article announcing the mission. How will you proceed?

Scenario 5: Dressing Right

You are a health care provider, and you are planning a fashion show for kindergartners, demonstrating proper clothing for various seasons and climates. You will provide a list of seasons and their characteristics, as well as a map of regions of the country and the various climate profiles for each. In addition, you will provide drawings and descriptions of the fashions and a master-of-ceremonies script for the fashion show. What will you do now?

Scenario 6: Online

You are a member of the Internet services board and you have been asked to develop a manual of tips for communicating via the Internet, including e-mails, Web sites, blogs, podcasts, wikis, and social networks. You will provide evidence of research, a role-play, a menu of Internet services, and an electronic presentation. What is next?

Scenario 7: School and More School

You are a board of education member in your district and have been asked to report on the concept of year-round schools." You must include both positive and negative aspects to be discussed, including research, evidence of community responses, and relevant conclusions. How will you conduct this investigation?

Scenario 8: Graffiti Gone

You are a park district official with a mandate from the mayor and the village board to deal with the prevalence of graffiti throughout the community. You will provide a site map, a solution to the graffiti, and a plan for executing this mission, with a timeline and a letter to citizens. How will you proceed?

Scenario 9: Decorating Madness

You are you! You have $200 to spend to redecorate your classroom. You will provide a budget, a scale drawing, comparative pricing, and an ad promoting your choices. What will you do?

In closing, the performance tasks cited above dictate the development of scoring rubrics for various selected elements. For example, the social studies area might want to do a rubric on the map or the historical references, science may need a rubric on science data, language arts may develop rubrics on a persuasive essay, technology on a Web search, and art on the brochure design. In any case, there is accountability written into these performance tasks in order to yield informative assessments for improved work.

■ □ ■ □ ■

Checklists. Checklists, as discussed earlier, are basic listings of the requirements for the product or performance. When checklists are derived from the actual wording of the standard (Burke, 2004), they are more likely to reflect the concepts and skills that students are expected to know and do. Yet checklists for products or performances often also include such global academic criteria as content, mechanics, research, organization, logical reasoning, accuracy, appearance, variety, and appeal. Eventually, this broad list of criteria is converted into a scoring rubric with descriptive quality indicators that create a range from poor to great.

Scoring Rubrics. Burke's method for turning a standard into a checklist and, in turn, turning the checklist into rubric with named criteria and quality indicators is discussed earlier in the previous chapter. Yet the full power of the process is not realized until that development is done with students. When they become immersed in the actual creation of the rubric, there is a rigor added to the rubric scoring process, and it becomes a more Rigorous Informative Assessment. It takes time and know-how to help students discern the essence of a standard or benchmark.

> **It takes time and know-how to help students discern the essence of a standard or benchmark.**

When students are asked to analyze the language of the standard, when they are expected to select key criteria, and when they are involved in creating parallel quality indicators, then and only then do they truly own the rubric. It's similar to when the students help decide the classroom rules: Once they decide, they really wrap their arms around the implementation and enforcement of those rules.

As an example, the following is a social studies standard:

> *Student Learning Standard: Students will understand world history and its relationship to current events.*
>
> *Analysis: Language of the Standard*

■ □ ■ □ ■

Social studies, world history, relationship, current events

Development of Criteria

World events, current events, logical relationship

Rubric Development With Quality Indicators

The teacher explains to the students that one of the formative assessment pieces will consist of a portfolio of work for the unit.

Based on that assessment, students are to develop a scoring rubric for the portfolio so they will be acutely aware of the expectations and requirements. After much discussion, they decide on three criteria and four levels of quality for each criterion. What follows is their resulting rubric for the social studies portfolio.

Social Studies World History Unit Portfolio: Scoring Rubric

World History Portfolio	Developing	Competent	Proficient	Above and Beyond
Targeted and appropriate world history and current events content	Little evidence of relationship of world events to current events	Sufficient evidence of relationship of world events to current	Much evidence of relationship of world events to current	Overwhelming evidence of relationship of world events to current
Evidence of multimodal learning	Little evidence of more than a singular modality employed	Evidence of at least three modalities in finished portfolio	Many modalities evidenced in the work represented in the portfolio	Highly creative use of modalities evidenced in actual presentation material and in the portfolio development itself

World History Portfolio	Developing	Competent	Proficient	Above and Beyond
Reflections on each item selected and included in the portfolio	Reflections missing or not fully developed in terms of establishing relationship of history and today	Appropriate reflections on each item and sufficient relationship developed between	Exceptional reflections that illuminate the relationship between history and today	Insightful reflections that intensify understanding of the relationship between history and today

Grading Practices

An astonishing shift is occurring not only in the literature, but also in the classrooms across North America. This shift is dramatic in its nature, as it begins the process of dethroning the "Almighty Grade" as the center of the kingdom of the classroom. It is a groundbreaking movement that calls for a revolution of sorts, as the academic community reexamines past practices about grades, grading, and the perennial green grade book.

This shift is dramatic in its nature, as it begins the process of dethroning the "Almighty Grade" as the center of the kingdom of the classroom.

In this section on Rigorous Informative Assessment tools, the discussion addresses gray areas that surround the grading issue, "traffic light" grading, grade books, including electronic grade books and their benefits for informing instruction, and finally, how traditional grade books are being used differently and what some view as radically changing ideas about grading practices.

Informative Grading

There is a gray area that surrounds the grading issue. This ambiguity is the controversy surrounding the use and

There is a gray area that surrounds the grading issue.

abuse of grades and grading practices. It revolves around the idea of whether the practices are used to punish students, rather than to support student learning.

This argument sets the precedent for revisiting grading practices. There is emerging evidence that grades and current grading practices tend to demoralize or lift student morale, depending on where the student falls on the grading chart. The literature cites questionable, and sometimes detrimental, effects that occur when grades are used as the final word (Black & Wiliam, 1998; Stiggins, 2007; Reeves, 2008; Guskey, 2007). First, the administration of grades is overemphasized and overshadows grading's original purpose, to give meaningful feedback for students to act on. Second, traditional grading, which compares student achievement, creates a competitive atmosphere among students rather than encouraging the focus on personal improvement. Third, when a grade is assigned to a paper, students don't give the accompanying comment any weight at all. Fourth, when grades are used, the focus is on the deficit area rather than on the strengths. Fifth, grading seems to keep students focusing on "doing well" and "getting a good grade," rather than focusing on what they are actually learning.

For those who will rebut this argument with the idea that grades are needed as consequences for students who are not doing the work or handing in the homework, the question that surfaces is, "What is the real goal of grades in schooling? Punishment or information? Grades do not motivate student learning" (Guskey, 2007). In fact, grades are more likely to demoralize students as they see the failures repeat over and over again. As educators, we must find ways to break the cycle of failure. One way is to revise grading practices to place the focus, front and center, on providing feedback through commentary and dialogue that provide actionable data.

Comments should give strengths and weaknesses. They should provide guidance for improvement. While changing the grading practices seems rigorous and radical, the commentary for improvement is what moves the student forward in the learning. If they don't value the comments when a numerical grade is given, teachers must begin to consider under what circumstances, and how often, they will give a grade and, in turn, when they will provide informative comments instead.

> **Comments should give strengths and weaknesses.**

Traffic Light Grading

One alternative to the traditional grade book is the traffic light grading strategy (Clymer & Wiliam, 2006). It consists of three assessment levels that simulate the traffic light: green, yellow, and red. As the teacher proceeds with standards-based lessons, student proficiencies are recorded using the traffic lights:

> Green—2 points, Mastery (consistently meets and often exceeds)
>
> Yellow—1 point, Developing (regularly meets the content standard)
>
> Red—0 points, Beginning or Below Basic (beginning to, and occasionally does, meet the content standards, or the student is not meeting standards)

The final grade is determined by the aggregate level of proficiency in the sum of the content standards. A test may also be used to verify the level of mastery.

Grade Books

Electronic Grade Books

Interestingly, the green grade book has almost met its demise by the intrusion of the electronic grade book. After all, the electronic version of the grade book offers such phenomenal benefits: accessibility, flexibility, timeliness, and ease of use. Electronic grade books make the data readily accessible to teachers, of course, but also to students and even to parents. These computer models of recording grades offer total flexibility in pulling specific data on a student, a class, across classes, across buildings, and even across districts. Electronic grade books are definite time savers for all stakeholders in increasingly busy schedules. Last but not least, the electronic versions of grade books are so very easy to use and to maintain.

Evolving Grading Practices

While the electronic grade book is gaining recognition as a highly functional Rigorous Informative Assessment tool, the traditional grade and grading techniques are under fire. The battles are being fought over the use of grades and grading practices as merely final judgments of student work. The shift, rather, is to view grades as indicators of what students know and do not know, to use grades as signals for supporting students' learning assets and deficits (O'Connor, 2002; Reeves, 2008; Guskey, 2007; Tomlinson, 2007; Black & Wiliam, 1998; Stiggins, 2007; and Popham, 2006).

Color-Coded Grade Books

An alternative to the traditional grade book practice of simply recording the grades is one that uses a coding technique to move the focus from a final grade (representing student learning), to a coded grade (informing student progress). In Figure 3.1, the grade book has added color-coding to indicate the level of student learning and understanding.

The green coding indicates mastery, the yellow indicates some misunderstandings or inaccuracies that

Figure 3.1

	A	B	C	D Int/Const step grphs	E Int.myst gtph	F Use % 0	G Find equiv names	H Ident. Landmks	I Calc/ Und mn	J Int/make line grph	K Int/make bar grph	L Grade
2			Unit	1	1	1	1	1	1	1	1	
3	Firstname	Lastname	Lesson	7	2	8	3	2	4	5	6	
4	JAMES	ALLEN		2	2	2	2	2	1	1	0	B
5	LIAM	AYEARS		2	2	2	0	1	1	0	1	C
6	LEE	BALDWIN		1	2	2	2	2	1	1	0	B
7	EMMA	BETTANY		2	2	1	2	2	2	1	1	B
8	LEAH	BIRCH		2	1	2	2	1	1	0	0	C
9	ROBERT	BURNS		2	2	1	0	1	1	0	0	C
10	DAVID	COBERN		2	2	2	2	2	1	0	1	B
11	SIMON	CREASEY		1	2	2	2	1	1	0	0	C
12	HANNAH	DARBY		1	2	2	2	1	2	1	1	B
13	LUKE	EASTWOOD		1	2	1	1	2	1	0	0	C
14	MARK	FERGUSON		2	2	2	2	2	2	0	1	A
15	SARAH	FORBES		1	0	1	1	2	1	0	0	C
16	MARK	GOODGER		2	2	2	2	2	2	2	1	A
17	MARK	HALL		1	2	2	2	2	2	2	1	A

■ Green   □ Yellow   ■ Red

need attention, and the red signals the teacher that these students need real and immediate intervention. While the grade book is still utilized, the focus is now on signaling and improving learning quality, rather than on the final stopping point.

No Zeros! No Averages! No "Killer Assignments"!

Reeves (2008) advocates against three specific teacher grading behaviors that are commonly used, yet proven to provide no real informative assessment data for students to act on to improve their understanding. His plea is passionate, yet reasoned. He calls for a moratorium on the use of zeros, averaging, and "killer projects."

The case is made for not putting zeros in the grade book for missing work. The goal of homework is

The case is made for not putting zeros in the grade book for missing work.

understood to be targeted and meaningful practice to solidify learning. Instead of giving the student a zero, give them a placeholder and require the student to do the work. This may mean providing a peer tutor, a homework help line, or even a homework haven within the school. But in any case, it seems better to set the bar for all students to complete the assigned work.

Reeves makes the case that the averaging of all scores throughout the term may actually punish the student with a lower grade, even if he has mastered the material later in the term. One cannot assume that learning early in the term is as important as the level of learning later in the semester. Now, while readers may not initially agree with these ideas, as they may seem too radical for traditionally conservative schools, it is time for all of the school personnel to visit some of these ideas and begin thinking about the real impact of grades.

A final concern that Reeves highlights is the typical use of a single project that carries great weight in the grading process. Sometimes the project, paper, lab, or performance is worth 25% to 40% of the grade. He calls this the "semester killer," for obvious reasons. This one assignment is so heavily rated over other class work that this one grade can make or break the student's grade for that class.

Electronic Test Creation Software

Software is plentiful, easily accessible, and even more easily implemented for staff members interested in this kind of technical help. They can readily plug in their content and create viable and reliable tests that yield viable and reliable data on student learning.

Test Creation Software

While Scantron machines have been in schools for some time, the next generation of assessment scoring technology is finally making it to many teachers' desks. Test creation and scoring software like AccelTest (Renaissance Learning) now allows teachers to design, score, and analyze assessments with greater efficiency than ever before. Nearly all of these systems provide item analysis, and many allow teachers to include references to state standards. They help teachers by allowing them to efficiently analyze their own assessment as well as track student performance data over time.

At the heart of Rigorous Informative Assessment, these types of software allow teachers to use summative assessment data in more formative manners—to make their summative assessments informative. Stiggins (2007) proposes a method of using a summative test formatively. He presents a scenario in which students are led through the process of analyzing their performance on a math test. Using a worksheet, they note their correct and incorrect answers, the reasons for missing problems (e.g., careless mistake or true lack of understanding), and then they link the problems to individual math concepts. Through this exercise, students might find that they missed several problems from simple mistakes and that all of the other problems missed relate to one or more topics. The teacher would then provide additional learning experiences and an alternate form of the test on which students could regain lost points.

Conceptually this sounds ideal. In terms of execution, it could be quite difficult. The teacher has to facilitate the hand analysis of test results, the additional learning experiences, and the re-testing. With test generation software, the test analysis is automatic, saving valuable time that could be used in other steps of this process.

Techniques

Higher-Order Thinking

The concept of higher-order thinking appears in every set of student learning standards, in every state in the union, in every curriculum in the world. The call for robust, rich, and authentic integrated projects and performances is critical to the high quality education aspired to by the founders of our educational system. In every schoolhouse and classroom in this nation, higher-order thinking reigns supreme. It is identified, named, pointed to, pointed out, and point taken that higher-order thinking is the common thread throughout all content and contexts.

More specifically, higher-order thinking is about macro-skills and micro-skills. It is about problem solving, decision making, and creative ideation. It is about predicting, inferring, and drawing conclusions, and it is also about comparing and contrasting, as well as analyzing and evaluating. In short, higher-order thinking is about thinking first, and being mindful about that thinking secondly. It is about reason and logic. It is about inductive and deductive lessons. Higher-order thinking is about honing the cognitive skills and abilities of our young people to prepare them for the 21st century.

Inductive Lesson

> **Often, higher-order thinking is embedded in the design of the actual lesson.**

Often, higher-order thinking is embedded in the design of the actual lesson. If it is structured as an inductive lesson, the activities move from specific facts and details to the general concept.

To illustrate in the clearest way the difference between structuring an inductive lesson versus a deductive lesson, a brief example will suffice. When teaching about magnets, the teacher would design a lab setting with lots of supplies and materials. Students would be directed to test various items with a set of magnets, to try to determine the law of attraction by what they observe in their experimentation.

The inductive model calls for trial and error. It is the life-learning model that one sees in young children, as they test and try out everything in their grasp until they can determine what fits the slot and what does not. The higher-order thinking triggered by this kind of discovery lesson involves the use of all senses, analysis, evaluation, hypotheses, and prediction, making inferences and drawing conclusions. Higher-order thinking is indeed the order of the day. This kind of investigative task, this kind of inquiry learning, provides the needed framework to observe and note the kinds of thinking unleashed by students as they problem solve and make critical decisions.

The inductive model calls for trial and error.

Deductive Lesson

On the other hand, if a lesson is structured as a deductive lesson, the activities move from the general concept to the specific facts and details. In that same context of a lesson on magnets, magnetic forces and magnetic pull, the teacher might start with the leading concept that magnets attract metal. Then, using the rule of magnetic attraction, students would test the law of attraction with various materials and substances. In this case, the deductive model also elicits student thinking of the highest order. This lesson design would require students to hypothesize, observe, compare and contrast, rank and order, determine generalities and cause and effect. In the deductive lesson design, generalizations are given, and they govern the task as it unfolds. Again, these are rigorous models of informative assessment that provide fertile ground for observational data about student reasoning and logical thinking.

In the deductive lesson design, generalizations are given, and they govern the task as it unfolds.

Tests, Test Questions, and Test Analysis

In addition to inductive and deductive lesson designs that encourage higher-order thinking, the actual construction of test questions, the structure, format, and utilization of the tests themselves, and the examination of student work provide other valued techniques that provide Rigorous Informative Assessment. While these are traditionally considered assessment instruments, they easily make the transition to instructional tools and techniques that are available to teachers to inform their practices.

Ungraded Practice Test

One method of Rigorous Informative Assessment is using sample tests to practice test-taking strategies. These sample tests provide question prototypes for students to use as practice tests. In one effective model, the teacher provides a sample test that requires a constructed response. Students respond to the questions in pencil and hand in the completed papers.

Then, instead of simply grading the paper, the teacher hands back the papers, and simultaneously shows students a quality-constructed response. In turn, students check their responses and determine which elements they have included and which they have not.

In a different color pen, the students add the needed elements to move the response from incomplete to a complete and comprehensive response. In this way, students actually get to see what a quality response looks like, instead of repeating the same mistakes and continually getting partial credit for an unfinished response. Over time, they learn to include the key elements needed for a good grade on the response question because they now know what it looks like and how to do it.

In this example, the tests are used to improve student performance by truly informing them on the specifics they need to increase their ratings. This kind of analysis with practice tests takes time and energy to do, yet the student improvement that results seems to indicate that the effort is warranted.

Examining Tests and Student Work Samples

There is a wonderful technique that is available to teachers to inform their practice. Although it is placed in the Rigorous Informative Assessment category, it is a method that is well worth the effort. The strategy is called "examining student work," and it involves a collaborative examination of a selected student assignment.

Simply described, teachers on the team actually do the student assignment first. They then select random samples of student work (or selected papers from a high-, middle-, or low-achieving student. They proceed to examine and rate the papers individually. After the rating process is completed, the team looks at all of the papers, analyzes and prioritizes them through discussion and debate. Eventually the team uses the results of this examination process to create a scoring rubric with criteria and indicators of quality.

This process provides insight and information to teachers about teacher expectations, the nature of the assignment and its strengths and weaknesses, and student reasoning. The qualitative data gleaned from this process live on as teachers apply this information to future assignments and tests.

Rating Work Samples

Each of us remembers the following conversation: We were talking with friends about a new teacher or professor, reflecting on grades early on in the semester,

**"I just don't know
what she wants."**

and lamenting, "I just don't know what she
wants." Have you had this conversation? And
can you see how a comment like this has no
place in ideal classroom assessment?

Additionally, at key instructional points, we ask
students to produce work that is utterly foreign to them.
Most students had never seen a lab report when their
science teacher called upon them to write one. Few
students have read research papers before writing one or
been to a science fair before crafting a science project. In
short, "Low achievement is often the result of students
failing to understand what is expected of them" (Black &
Wiliam, 1998).

Numerous assessment authors focus in on this
phenomenon and seek ways to make "learning objectives
and [our] criteria for success transparent to students"
(Leahy, Lyon, Thompson, & Wiliam, 2005). Perhaps one
of the simplest is to "circulat[e] work samples . . . in view
of prompting a discussion about quality" (De Bono,
1992, p. 21).

While it might take some time for teachers to save up
a collection of work samples, it is time well spent. We
should particularly note that for this endeavor to be most
effective, samples of varying quality are necessary. While
many teachers hold on to stellar work samples, few retain
less than satisfactory samples.

> *Initially, a teacher might want to choose four or five
> exemplars at very different levels of quality, to get students to
> focus on broad criteria for quality," then "as students get
> more skilled . . . have a number of samples of similar quality
> to force students to be more critical and reflective. (Leahy
> et al., p. 21)*

Ask students to rate the work samples, using a rubric
where appropriate. If they rate correctly, they are ready to
produce work on their own. If not, we must focus in on

their discussions about the work samples. What do the lower quality work samples lack, or the best samples contain, that they fail to see? Listening to these discussions will inform our practice and help us know what we need to teach our students to see.

Summative Assessments as Formative Assessments

An interesting, and not entirely unique, method of implementing Rigorous Informative Assessment is the use of traditional assessments as informative assessments. While these traditional assessments are often regarded as summative in nature, they offer rich opportunities for assessing in more formative ways. While a philosophical shift between traditional and novel uses of summative assessments may be necessary, the fact remains that there is the possibility of using a summative assessment in a formative manner.

Within the context of this idea of using summative assessments to inform instructional practice, there are several familiar techniques that are ripe for the picking. They include the use of data and the use of item analyses. Both of these tools are highly effective to inform instructional practices.

Data

In using traditionally generated data that are both quantitative and qualitative, hard and soft data, numerical and narrative data, and graphed and anecdotal data, the possibilities for informing students and teachers about student understanding is phenomenal. With this Rigorous Informative Assessment technique, data are a centerpiece of differentiated classroom practices.

While some kinds of data are used on a daily basis, there is a more rigorous data debate that occurs periodically throughout the term. This is a more deliberate and more comprehensive examination of data that determines key instructional decisions for teachers and teacher teams.

To explore how this rigorous look at data occurs, there are three elements that seem pertinent. As data take front and center in the classroom, teachers embrace three components: data, dialogue, and decisions (Schmoker, 1996)—more specifically, managed data, meaningful team dialogue, and measureable goals. This process, summarized as data, dialogue, and decisions, occurs periodically in schools.

The first step is the availability of "managed data" from standardized tests, benchmark tests, or even end-of-course tests. This data often comes to the teams as disaggregated data, separating subskills, gender, grade levels, and students for closer examination.

Next, the data are analyzed by meaningful teams or teams of teachers working with the same group of kids. These might be grade level, department, or core middle level teams, or professional learning communities. In their sessions, they use certain questioning protocols to work through the data. The traditional questions fall into four categories to keep the team in to guide the dialogue in a problem-solving mode. The four questions are (1) what? (2) what else? (3) so what? and (4) now what?

The final step, following the analysis and dialogue, involves setting a measureable goal and deciding on an instructional intervention to guarantee that the goal is met. The goal is sometimes called a SMART goal, which acronym spells out specific elements needed in the goal statement: Specific, Measureable, Attainable, Result-oriented, Time-bound.

■□■□■

Specific—Name the numbers, percentages, or gains expected

Measurable—Devise a way to measure the goal named

Attainable—Be reasonable and real; the goal must be achieved

Result-oriented—Determine the results that were targeted

Time-bound—Set a date to check results, report back, and revise for next steps

Once the goal is determined, a specific intervention must be implemented. That is the key to accomplishing the goal. Currently, many schools are using the rigors of this assessment model to inform their practice. Yet the weak link in the process is, more often than not, in targeting an intervention that is performed with fidelity.

> **The weak link in the process is, more often than not, in targeting an intervention that is performed with fidelity.**

An example of a SMART goal: The third graders in the bottom quartile will increase comprehension scores by 25% by the end of the next ten-week marking period. All identified students will receive skill building in seven comprehension skills, thirty minutes a day, every day of the week. The seven target skills include accessing prior knowledge, finding important themes, asking questions while reading, visualizing, making inferences, summarizing, and metacognitive reflection. Student skill work will be recorded daily in a "Comprehension Skills Log."

Notice that the goal is supported very specifically, including many details of the intervention. In addition, fidelity to implementation is advocated through the log.

While this is just a glimpse of the data process that is a Rigorous Informative Assessment technique, there is much written on this strategy. A resource that delineates this entire process in detail is the *In a Nutshell* book *Data! Dialogue! Decisions! The Data Difference* by Pete and Sambo (2004).

Item Analysis

Another effective Rigorous Informative Assessment technique is called item analysis. In this strategy, test items are examined to reveal underlying language that is called *robust distracters*. Robust distracters consist of language or responses that are confusing to students and that may lead them in the wrong direction. Particular focus is given to the incorrect answer options, also referred to as *distracters* or *decoy answers*. By examining the incorrect answers that students provide or choose, we can often find insight into their thinking, thereby revealing a clear direction for subsequent instruction.

Robust distracters consist of language or responses that are confusing to students and that may lead them in the wrong direction.

Item Analysis 1. Question:

3 inches

2 inches

What is the area of this rectangle?

a. 6 inches

b. 6 square inches

c. 10 inches

d. 9 square inches

a. incorrect unit; b. correct answer; c. perimeter; d. applying area of a square formula using the value from the longest side

What else do the problem and other responses tell us about student thinking?

Item Analysis 2. Algebra

$4a = 24$

$a + b = 12$

Find a and b.

Correct answer: a and b both equal 6

In terms of algebra, this statement is correct; a and b both equal 6. However, students new to algebra, not having any confidence in their ability, will work the problem, find the correct answer, and say to themselves, "I must have done something wrong." They don't think a and b can both equal 6. They don't understand that letters are merely fill-ins for unknowns in algebra and two unknowns can be the same value. They expect the problem to be harder than it really is; they are looking for a trick.

There is a trick, but it's a trick answer.

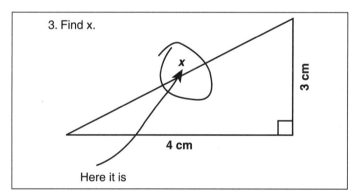

3. Find x.

x

3 cm

4 cm

Here it is

Item Analysis 3. Question:

"He ran like the wind" is an example of

a. a simile

b. a metaphor

c. personification

d. hyperbole

a. correct answer; b. a common incorrect answer as students often have trouble distinguishing between similes (comparisons using "like" or "as") and metaphors

Item Analysis 4. (Rigorous and Robust Distracters). Question:

What was the first English settlement in the United States?

a. Roanoke Island, NC

b. St. Augustine, FL

c. Jamestown, VA

d. Plymouth, MA

Correct answer: Roanoke Island, NC (also known as "The Lost Colony")

Jamestown, VA—First *permanent* English settlement

St. Augustine, FL—First permanent *Spanish* settlement

Plymouth, MA—Another early English settlement, a likely answer.

Item Analysis 5. Math Computation

What do you see? What is happening?

$$\begin{array}{r} 17 \\ + 54 \\ \hline 17 \end{array}$$

17 is the wrong answer!

Look again. What patterns do you see?

$$\begin{array}{cccccc}
17 & 34 & 76 & 37 & 28 & 45 \\
+54 & 28 & 13 & 25 & 43 & 62 \\
\hline
17 & 17 & 17 & 17 & 17 & 17
\end{array}$$

What is happening? Correct Analysis

1. Directionality (adding across then totaling)

$$\begin{array}{rl}
17 & = 8 \\
+54 & = 9 \\
\hline
17 & 17
\end{array}$$

2. No concept of addition (add gets more)
3. Place value
4. Pattern of 17 may confuse

Analysis	Intervention
Directionality	Manipulatives
Place value	Paper guide
No concept	Arrows
of addition	Tens groupings
	Graph paper
	Re-teach

Notice in the analysis/intervention chart that there are a number of errors in the student's thinking about the addition problem. First, he is misusing directionality by adding horizontally rather than vertically. Next, he does not have a correct sense of place value as indicated by his response, nor does he have an understanding of the concept of addition. If he understood addition, he would realize that the answer to the problem should be larger than the two numbers he was adding. Notice that item analyses yield many clues and cues to faulty student thinking. While the reasoning sometimes seems logical, it often has a fatal flaw caused by a robust distracter. When teacher teams take the time to analyze test items or work sample items, they often gain great insights into the way students are thinking about the concepts or ideas they have been working on. While it does take dedicated time and deliberate, intentional focus by the team, the benefits are usually well worth the information that emerges.

Tasks

Grades: "Crime and Punishment" or "A Personal Best"

As an innovative approach to Rigorous Informative Assessment, ask a partner or a team of fellow teachers to consider the three principles of innovative grading practices, advocated by Reeves (2008), as discussed earlier in this chapter: no zeros; no averaging; no "killer assignment." The following is what the team might do.

Keep two sets of grades for one class or one subject, for one term.

Keep two sets of grades for one class or one subject, for one term. Keep one set of grades with the traditional methods of using (1) zeros for work not turned in, (2) averaged grades for the term, and (3) the weight of the semester project as usual (25% or whatever percentage allotted).

Then keep a second set of grades and follow these simple rules on the second set of grades:

1. Do not use "zero" for work not turned in. Require that the work be done and turned in, and facilitate that requirement.

2. Don't average the grades for the semester. Give more consideration to the quality and grades of the work later in the term when students have had time to learn.

3. Don't weight a semester assignment so heavily that it outweighs the daily work, periodic quizzes, and so on. Perhaps give incremental grading on phases of the project, as it unfolds.

Talk with team members about the title of the activity. Now compare and contrast the two sets of grades and discuss fully in a debriefing with team members who have also tried this same experiment. Unpack the idea of grades that punish versus grades that motivate and inspire a student's personal best. Talk about the real purpose of schooling, grading, and grades. Have a philosophical look at doing grading a different way. Think about the implications of this idea. Decide what the next step might be.

Tips

Tip 1: Start slowly.

Tip 2: Address one new thing at a time.

Tip 3: Work collaboratively. Use your professional learning communities, your department teams, or your grade-level or core middle school team. Let the synergy of the group work carry this forward as rigorous investigations for professional growth.

Tip 4: Use technology software whenever possible to guide the process. There are lots of options to make the work easier and more available, accessible and changeable.

Tip 5: Continue the journey and add a little bit of finesse along the way. Make it a mission to learn more tools and techniques to inform your professional practice.

Tip 6: Embrace Rigorous Informative Assessment tools and techniques as part and parcel of your professional learning. The insights they yield are well worth the effort.

Chapter 4

Closure

Couched within the writings of Black, Wiliam, Stiggins, and many others is the serious consideration of the motivational impact that assessment strategies have on students. Indeed, this is a very serious consideration.

The work of psychologist Carol Dweck (2007) offers many insights in this area. She has focused much of her research and writing on "attribution theory," studying how and where students attribute blame when they fail. She contends that there are stark differences between how high-achieving and low-achieving students perceive, and ultimately deal with, failure and that a significant key to finding success with many students is to help our low-achieving students change their failure paradigms to ones more closely resembling those of high-achieving students.

Dweck presents two mind-sets or models of intelligence. Some students hold a "growth mind-set," believing that "intellectual ability is something they can develop through effort." Others hold a "fixed mind-set," believing that "their intellectual ability is a fixed trait" (pp. 34–35).

She notes that these mind-sets arise from the types of praise we offer students. "Praising students' intelligence," thereby promoting a fixed mind-set, "gives them a short burst of pride, followed by a long string

> **Some students hold a "growth mind-set," believing that "intellectual ability is something they can develop through effort." Others hold a "fixed mind-set," believing that "their intellectual ability is a fixed trait."**
>
> Dweck, 2007, pp. 34–35

of negative consequences," because, when faced with a challenge, students with a fixed mind-set typically lose motivation quickly and shy away from challenges. "They are also afraid of effort because effort makes them feel dumb. They believe that if you have the ability, you shouldn't need effort" (p. 35).

In contrast, students with a growth mind-set "care about learning. When they make a mistake or exhibit a deficiency, they correct it. For them, effort is a positive thing; it ignites their intelligence and causes it to grow. In the face of failure, these students escalate their efforts and look for new learning strategies" (p. 36).

As opposed to offering any praise related to intelligence (e.g., "You're really smart with this type of work"), Dweck suggests that we should offer "'process' praise (praise for engagement, perseverance, strategies, improvement, and the like)," which will "[foster] hardy motivation" and a solid growth mind-set.

Process praise, Dweck suggests, sounds like the following:

- You really studied for your English test, and your improvement shows it. You read the material over several times, outlined it, and attested yourself on it. That really worked!

- I like the way you treated all kinds of strategies on that math problem until you finally got it.

- It was a long, hard assignment, but you stuck to it and got it done. You stayed at your desk, kept up your concentration, and kept working. That's great!

- I like that you took on that challenging project for your science class. It will take a lot of work—doing the research, designing the machine, buying the parts, and building it. You're going to learn a lot of great things. (Dweck, 2007, p. 37)

In closing, this "attribution theory" offers a compelling argument for informative assessments—routine, reflective, and rigorous assessments—that create inspiration and motivation for students. Assessments that inform are assessments that foster student improvement rather than student impoverishment.

> *None of these ideas is new, and a large and growing research base shows that implementing them yields substantial improvement in student learning. So why are these strategies and techniques not practiced more widely? The answer is that knowing about these techniques and strategies is one thing; figuring out how to make them work in your own classroom is something else.*
>
> *Many of these techniques require only subtle changes in practice, yet research on the underlying strategies suggests that they have a high "gearing"—meaning that these small changes in practice can leverage large gains in student learning. (Leahy, Lyon, Thompson, & Wiliam, 2005, p. 20)*

Afterword

In closing, the idea of assessment of, for, and as learning (Tomlinson, 2007) is the critical understanding teachers must come to. Assessment of learning sees assessment as judging learning. Assessment for learning sees teachers informing teaching. Assessment as learning sees assessment informing learning.

References

Assessment Training Institute. (2003). *Assessment for learning: A hopeful vision of the future* [Motion picture]. (Available from the Assessment Training Institute, Portland, OR)

Black, P., & Wiliam, D. (1998). Inside the black box: Raising standards through classroom assessment. *Phi Delta Kappan, 80*(2), 139–148.

Black, P., Harrison, C., Lee, C., Marshall, B., & Wiliam, D. (2003). *Assessment for learning: Putting it into practice.* Berkshire, England: Open University Press.

Burke, K. (2004). *Performance assessment: Evidence of learning.* Chicago: Fogarty & Associates.

Clymer, J. B., & Wiliam, D. (2006). Improving the way we grade science. *Educational Leadership, 64*(4), 36–42.

Costa, A., & Kallick, B. (Eds.). (2000). *Discovering & exploring habits of mind.* Alexandria, VA: Association for Supervision and Curriculum Development.

De Bono, E. (1992). *Six thinking hats for schools: K–12 resource book.* Des Moines, IA: McQuaig Group.

Dweck, C. S. (2007). The perils and promises of praise. *Educational Leadership 65*(2), 34–39.

Gardner, H. (1983). *Frames of mind: The theory of multiple intelligences.* New York: Basic Books.

Guskey, T. R. (2003). How classroom assessments improve learning. *Educational Leadership, 60*(5), 6–11.

Guskey, T. R. (2007). The rest of the story. *Educational Leadership 65*(4), 28–35.

Johnson, D. W., & Johnson, R. T. (1988). *Circles of learning: Cooperation in the classroom.* Alexandria, VA: Association for Supervision and Curriculum Development.

Kerman, S. (1979). Teacher expectations and student achievement. *Phi Delta Kappan, 60*(10), 716–18.

Kozol, J. (2007). *Letters to a young teacher.* New York: Three Rivers Press.

Leahy, S., Lyon, C., Thompson, M., & Wiliam, D. (2005). Classroom assessment: Minute by minute, day by day. *Educational Leadership, 63*(3), 18–24.

Marzano, R., Pickering, D., & McTighe, J. (1993). *Assessing Student Outcomes: Performance Assessment Using the Dimensions of Learning Model.* Alexandria, VA: Association for Supervision and Curriculum Development.

O'Connor, K. (2002). *How to grade for learning: Linking grades to standards.* Thousand Oaks, CA: Corwin.

Pete, B., & Sambo, C. (2004). *Data! Dialogue! Decisions! The data difference.* Thousand Oaks, CA: Corwin.

Popham, W. J. (2006). All about accountability/Those [fill in the blank] tests! *Educational Leadership, 63*(8), 85–86.

Reeves, D. B. (2008). Leading to change/Effective grading practices. *Educational Leadership, 65*(5), 85–87.

Schmoker, M. J. (1996). *Results: The key to continuous school improvement.* Alexandria, VA: Association for Supervision and Curriculum Development.

Stiggins, R. (2007). Assessment through the student's eyes. *Educational Leadership, 64*(8), 22–26.

Swearingen, R. (2002). *A primer: Diagnostic, formative, & summative assessment.* Retrieved March 8, 2009, from http://slackernet.org/assessment.htm

Tomlinson, C. A. (2007). Learning to love assessment. *Educational Leadership 65*(4), 8–13.

Tyler, R. W. (1949). *Basic principles of curriculum and instruction.* Chicago: University of Chicago Press.

Wiliam, D. (2007). Changing classroom practice. *Educational Leadership 65*(4), 36–42.

Wiggins, G. (1998). *Educative assessment.* San Francisco: Jossey-Bass.

Wiggins, G., & McTighe, J. (2005). *Understanding by design* (2nd ed.). Alexandria, VA: Association for Supervision and Curriculum Development.

Resources and Further Reading

Andrade, H. (2007). Self-Assessment through rubrics. *Educational Leadership 65*(4) 60–63.

Assessment Resource Bank. (2001). *Formative assessment.* Retrieved October 14, 2008, from http://arb.nzcer.org.nz/nzcer3/furform.htm

Bambrick-Santoyo, P. (2007). Data in the driver's seat. *Educational Leadership 65*(4) 43–47.

Barton, P. E. (2007). The right way to measure growth. *Educational Leadership 65*(4), 70–73.

Bloom, B. S., Hastings, J . T., & Madaus, G. F. (1971). *Handbook on formative and summative evaluation of student learning.* New York: McGraw Hill.

Brookhart, S. M. (2007). Feedback that fits. *Educational Leadership 65*(4) 54–59.

Brookhart, S. M. (1999). [Review of book by G. Wiggins, *Educative assessment: Designing assessments to inform and improve student performance.*] Retrieved March 9, 2009, from http://edrev.asu.edu/reviews/rev50.htm

Burns, M. (2005). Looking at how students reason. *Educational Leadership 63*(3), 26–31.

Chappuis, J. (2005). Helping students understand assessment. *Educational Leadership 63*(3), 39–43.

Chappuis, S., & Chappuis, J. (2007). The best value in formative assessment. *Educational Leadership 65*(4), 14–18.

Delaware Student Testing Program, Delaware Department of Education. (2008). *Item sampler, released mathematics items, Grades 4 and 5.* Publication No. 95–01/08/01/09. Retrieved March 8, 2009, from http://www.doe.k12.de.us/aab/files/2008%20Math%20Item%20Sampler%20-%20GR4,5.pdf

Dicks, M. J. (2005). Show me the way. *Educational Leadership 63*(3) 78–80.

Dillon, A., & Gabbard, R. (1998). Hypermedia as an educational technology: A review of the quantitative research literature on learner comprehension, control, and style. *Review of Educational Research, 68*(3) 322–349.

Fisher, D., Grant, M., Frey, N., & Johnson. C. (2007). Taking formative assessment schoolwide. *Educational Leadership 65*(4) 64–68.

Fogarty, R. (1998). *Balanced assessment.* Thousand Oaks, CA: Corwin.

Fogarty, R. (1999). *How to raise test scores.* Thousand Oaks, CA: Corwin.

Fogarty, R. (2001). *Standards of learning: A blessing in disguise.* Chicago: Fogarty & Associates.

Fogarty, R., & Pete, B. (2005). *Test-taking strategies: Psst! Pass it on!* Chicago: Fogarty & Associates.

Guskey, T. R. (2005). Mapping the road to proficiency. *Educational Leadership 63*(3), 32–38.

Guskey, T. R. (April, 2005). *Formative classroom assessment and Benjamin S. Bloom: Theory, research and implications.* Paper presented at the annual meeting of the American Educational Research Association, Montreal, Quebec, Canada.

Herman, J. L., & Baker, E. L. (2005). Making benchmark testing work. *Educational Leadership 63*(3), 48–54.

Huhn, C. (2005). How many points is this worth? *Educational Leadership 63*(3), 81–82.

Johnson, D. W., & Johnson, R. T. (1995). Cooperative learning. In J. H. Block, S. T. Everson, and T. R. Guskey (Eds.), *School Improvement Programs* (pp. 25–56). New York: Scholastic.

Kellough, R. D., & Kellough, N. G. (1999). *Secondary school teaching: A guide to methods and resources: Planning for competence.* Upper Saddle River, NJ: Merrill.

McNamee, G. D., & Chen, J-Q. (2005). Dissolving the line between assessment and teaching. *Educational Leadership, 63*(3), 72–76.

Niguidula, D. (2005). Documenting learning with digital portfolios. *Educational Leadership 63*(3), 44–47.

Popham, W. J. (1999). *Classroom assessment: What teachers need to know* (2nd ed.). Needham Heights, MA: Allyn & Bacon.

Popham, W. J. (2007). Ask about accountability/How to play the appraisal game. *Educational Leadership 65*(4), 88–89.

Reeves, D. B. (2007). Leading to change/How do you sustain excellence? *Educational Leadership 65*(3), 86–87.

Shepard, L. A. (2005). Linking formative assessment to scaffolding. *Educational Leadership, 63*(3), 66–70.

Silver, H. F., Strong, R. W., & Perini, M. J. (2000). *So each may learn: Integrating learning styles and multiple intelligences.* Alexandria, VA: Association for Supervision and Curriculum Development.

Slavin, R. E. (1991). Synthesis of research on cooperative learning. *Educational Leadership 48*(5), 71–82.

Sternberg, R. J. (2007). Assessing what matters. *Educational Leadership, 65*(4), 20–26.

Stiggins, R. (2004). New assessment beliefs for a new school mission. *Phi Delta Kappan, 86*(1), 22–27.

Stiggins, R. (2005). From formative assessment to assessment FOR learning: A path to success in standards-based schools. *Phi Delta Kappan, 87*(4), 324–328.

Stiggins, R., & Chappuis, J. (2005). Using student-involved classroom assessment to close achievement gaps. *Theory Into Practice, 44*(1), 11–18.

Winger, T. (2005). Grading to communicate. *Educational Leadership, 63*(3), 61–65.

Index

■□■□■

CORWIN
A SAGE Company

The Corwin logo—a raven striding across an open book—represents the union of courage and learning. Corwin is committed to improving education for all learners by publishing books and other professional development resources for those serving the field of PreK–12 education. By providing practical, hands-on materials, Corwin continues to carry out the promise of its motto: **"Helping Educators Do Their Work Better."**